SRHE and Open University Press Imprint

General Editor: Heather Eggins

Current titles include:

David Warner and David Palfreyman (eds): *Higher Education Management of UK Higher Education*
Gareth Williams (ed): *The Enterprising University*
Diana Woodward and Karen Ross: *Managing Equal Opportunities in Higher Education*

Retention and Student Success in Higher Education

Mantz Yorke and Bernard Longden

Society for Research into Higher Education
& Open University Press

Open University Press
McGraw-Hill Education
McGraw-Hill House
Shoppenhangers Road
Maidenhead
Berkshire
England
SL6 2QL

email: enquiries@openup.co.uk
world wide web: www.openup.co.uk

First published 2004
Reprinted 2008

A catalogue record of this book is available from the British Library

ISBN-10: 0335 21274 3 (pb)   0335 21275 1 (hb)
ISBN-13: 978 0 335 212743 (pb)   978 0 335 21275 0 (hb)

Library of Congress Cataloging-in-Publication Data
CIP data applied for

Typeset by YHT Ltd
Printed in the UK by Bell & Bain Ltd., Glasgow

To present and future students
in higher education

Contents

viii   *Contents*

Contributors

John M. Braxton

John M. Braxton is Professor of Education in the Higher Education Leadership and Policy Program in the Department of Leadership, Policy and Organizations at Peabody College, Vanderbilt University, Nashville, Tennessee. His research interests centre on the college student experience, the sociology of the academic profession, and academic course-level processes. He has published extensively in refereed journals and contributed to book chapters in areas associated with his research interests. Professor Braxton serves as a Consulting Editor for the *Journal of Higher Education* and *Research in Higher Education*. He is the current President of the Association for the Study of Higher Education.

Ian A. Bunting

Ian Bunting was full-time Dean of the Faculty of Social Science at the University of Cape Town between 1987 and 1998. In 1999 he was seconded to the Higher Education Branch of the national Department of Education. He is now Acting Head of the Branch's higher education planning directorate.

Amy S. Hirschy

Amy S. Hirschy is a graduate doctoral research student at Vanderbilt University, Nashville, Tennessee, working with John Braxton on issues relating to the student experience. Prior to returning to study at Vanderbilt, Amy Hirschy worked as a college student services administrator for thirteen years. Grounded in that practical experience from within student administration, she now pursues research into college student experience in general and, more specifically, factors that positively and negatively influence students' educational persistence.

Richard James

Richard James is an Associate Professor in the Centre for the Study of Higher Education at the University of Melbourne. He has published widely on higher education access and participation, student decision-making during the transition to university, and quality assurance. In 2002, he conducted a national project on the assessment of student learning for the Australian Universities Teaching Committee.

Craig McInnis

Craig McInnis is Professor of Higher Education and Director of the Centre for the Study of Higher Education, the University of Melbourne. His most recent national projects include: studies of trends in the first year under-graduate experience; changing academic work roles in Australia; a review of factors contributing to student non-completion; and a study of the impact of part-time paid work on the full-time undergraduate experience.

Acknowledgements

We are grateful to the following for permission to reproduce the student quotations listed below.

The Universities and Colleges Admissions Service [UCAS], for those from Yorke (1999a).

Thomson Publishing Services, for those from Yorke (1999b).

Rhys Davies and Peter Elias for those from Davies and Elias (2003).

We are also grateful to the Higher Education Funding Council for England [HEFCE] for funding studies that we have undertaken on non-completion and student success. The opinions expressed in this book should not, of course, be taken as representing those of HEFCE.

Abbreviations

AIR	Association for Institutional Research (USA)
API	Age Participation Index (UK)
ASHE	Association for the Study of Higher Education (USA)
AUTC	Australian Universities Teaching Committee
BTEC	Business and Technology Education Council (UK)
CAE	College of Advanced Education (Aus)
CDP	Committee of Directors of Polytechnics (UK)
CEQ	Course Experience Questionnaire (Aus)
CSHE	Centre for the Study of Higher Education (Aus)
CVCP	Committee of Vice-Chancellors and Principals – now Universities UK
DEL	Department for Employment and Learning (Northern Ireland)
DENI	Department of Education in Northern Ireland
DEST	Department of Education, Science and Training (Aus)
DETYA	Department of Education, Training and Youth Affairs (Aus)
DfEE	Department for Education and Employment (UK)
DfES	Department for Education and Skills (UK)
GCCA	Graduate Careers Council of Australia
GNVQ	General National Vocational Qualification (UK)
HECS	Higher Education Contribution Scheme (Aus)
HEFCE	Higher Education Funding Council for England
HESA	Higher Education Statistics Agency (UK)
JPIWG	Joint Performance Indicator Working Group (UK)
NAO	National Audit Office (UK)
NCES	National Center for Educational Statistics (USA)
NCHEMS	National Center for Higher Education Management Systems (USA)
NCIHE	National Committee of Inquiry into Higher Education (UK)
OECD	Organisation for Economic Co-operation and Development
QAA	Quality Assurance Agency for Higher Education (UK)
RAE	Research Assessment Exercise (UK)

SES	Socio-economic status
SPU	Student Progress Unit (Aus)
SSR	Staff-Student Ratio
TAFE	Technical and Further Education (Aus)
UCAS	Universities and Colleges Admissions Service (UK)
UNS	Unified National System (Aus)
UUK	Universities UK (formerly CVCP)
VLE	Virtual Learning Environment

Prologue

The cusp of change

Student retention and attrition are of policy significance to higher education systems around the world. Governments want higher education to be as effective and efficient as possible, not only because of labour market considerations but also because they have to account to their publics for the investment that they have made on their publics' behalf. When students discontinue their studies involuntarily (because of academic failure or some precipitating cause that is not their responsibility) or more voluntarily, this can be construed in terms of inefficiency in the system. The Higher Education Funding Council for England (HEFCE) hints at this view in its publication of 'Projected learning outcomes and efficiencies' within the UK higher education sector (for example HEFCE 2002).

Retention and attrition are of obvious concern to institutions. Institutions signal in various ways their commitment to the students whom they enrol, and high levels of attrition inevitably raise questions about the fulfilment of that commitment. Keeping retention levels as high as possible is important because of the reputational benefit that accrues from the successes of their students, and because of the economic stability that a predictable student base engenders.

The international literature refers to concepts such as persistence, retention, completion, attrition, dropout, non-completion and the particularly pejorative 'wastage'. Many of these are managerially-oriented – not that there is anything wrong with a managerial perspective. However, a managerial perspective tends to lose sight of the student perspective that can be seen in 'persistence', 'completion' and 'success'.

In our view, the student perspective is at the heart of what Braxton (2000b) calls 'the student departure puzzle'. A lot depends, as we shall argue in the later chapters of this book, on the student's perception of their experience in higher education. This is affected by psychological, sociological and other influences, some of which are well beyond the powers of an institution. However, there are many ways in which an institution can influence a student's experience, to either their benefit or their detriment. In the UK, there has been a slight but, we believe, significant shift in thinking about matters relating to retention and completion – a growth in looking at the relevant issues from the perspective of their potential contribution to student success. Our book is on the cusp of this change.

Navigating this book

This book is arranged in two broad parts. The first five chapters are primarily concerned with higher education systems and their performance. The second five have as their main focus how institutions can help to increase the chances of students' success.

Chapter 1 sets the scene by locating retention, completion and success in their political context and by discussing the interests of three key stakeholders – students themselves, institutions and governments. Bearing in mind that some readers will be unfamiliar with all of the higher education systems of the four countries which are particularly featured in the book (South Africa, Australia, England and the United States), the second part of this chapter provides brief sketches by way of orientation. Chapter 2 illustrates the severe challenges faced by South Africa in the post-apartheid era: Bunting describes the size and shape of the national higher education system, and points to the stresses that make high levels of student success difficult to secure. McInnis and James describe in Chapter 3 the recent evolution of the Australian system and its efforts to ensure equitable participation. They draw on research findings relating to completion and to that critically important period in a student's engagement in higher education – the first year experience – and indicate some of the main reasons for discontinuation. These will have a familiar ring to readers in the UK. Chapter 4 takes a different slant, presenting a case study of the ways in which the parliamentary system has recently engaged with the linked issues of student funding, and access to, and retention and completion in, higher education in England. The last of the quintet, Chapter 5, examines performance indicators relating to retention and completion, and discusses what they reveal and what they do not. The chapter also includes a brief discussion of how the press handled the publication of the performance statistics for higher education in the UK.

Chapters 6 and 7 address the issue of theory relating to retention and student success. In Chapter 6 the argument is advanced that, whilst much of the theorizing about retention reflects sociological concerns, students' decision-making whether to persist or withdraw is fundamentally a matter of psychology (even though sociological issues may exert influence). Chapter 7, by Braxton and Hirschy, takes what might be termed the 'market leader' in theoretical formulation, Tinto's (1993) contribution, and subjects it to test. Whilst there is substantial empirical support for the positive effect on retention of aspects of 'social integration', the level of support in respect of 'academic integration' is much weaker.

Chapter 8 draws on two surveys of students who discontinued their studies in a range of English institutions, augmenting the general findings with illustrative quotations. A number of English institutions enrol a high proportion of students from disadvantaged backgrounds, with some achieving retention levels that are better than their demographic profiles would suggest. Chapter 9, based on interviews conducted in a range of these institutions, discusses the ways in which they are seeking to encourage student success 'against the demographic odds'. Chapter 10 consists of a series of broad suggestions as to how the chances of student success might be enhanced, drawing on theoretical and empirical material presented earlier in the book.

Those with an academic interest in retention and success will probably want to engage with the whole of this book, though they will also need to refer to a number of the sources that we have mentioned, since our intention has not been to produce a comprehensive study of the field – rather, the aim has been to produce a book that will be useful in a number of practical ways. Those with a preference for comparative study will probably find Chapters 2 to 5 of primary interest, whereas those whose interests lie towards the theoretical will probably wish to focus on Chapters 6 and 7. Those whose concerns are pragmatically oriented towards addressing the question 'What can we do in this institution to enhance retention and success?' will probably want to focus on Chapters 8 to 10 – though we hope that they will be tempted to work their way back through some of the earlier material as well, if only to track the sources of some of the suggestions we have made.

1
Setting the scene

Human capital and social justice

Governments around the world have adopted a 'human capital' approach
to higher education (Becker 1975), which can be summarized as seeing the
success of their national economies in terms of the degree to which the
labour force is educated. Nations differ, though, in the way in which their
higher education provision is structured. In the USA and in continental
Europe there are strong traditions of modes of education leading to
intermediate qualifications, whereas in England (until the recent introduction of Foundation Degrees[1]) there has been something of an 'academic drift' towards degrees and away from programmes aimed at
intermediate qualifications.

At the same time, there are social justice components to higher education
policy making. We note below policy concerns in different countries
regarding the inclusion of under-represented groups in higher education
(which, of course, has its human capital aspects as well).

Governments invest to varying extents in their higher education systems.
They therefore seek to ensure that they get the best return on their
investment, implying an interest in maximizing retention and completion.
The growth in the use of systems of quality assurance, and the use of performance indicators, can be seen as demonstrations of their interest.

Retention, completion and success

The importance of student success in higher education is incontestable,
whether one's standpoint is that of a student, a programme team, a
department, an institution, or a higher education system.[2] However, the
reason why success is important is coloured by the particular standpoint.

Retention and completion

Retention and attrition, like many terms in this field, are difficult to define once students move away from straightforward full-time engagement and spread out their studying over a period longer than that nominally expected for their programme. A pragmatic view has to be taken, such as is done by the HEFCE, which allows for a one-year gap when it computes progression rates.

Retention and attrition are 'supply-side' concepts, as to some extent is the completion of a programme of study. They are managerially-oriented, signalling a focus on the effectiveness and efficiency of an institution or a system. The relevant official statistics permit benchmarking

- against expected values, as is practised by the Funding Councils in the UK in the publication of national performance indicators (for example HEFCE 2002)
- against comparable (and sometimes very different) institutions
- against other national systems, as is exemplified in the relevant OECD tables (for example OECD 2002).

Likewise, the statistics available from institutional management systems allow intra-institutional benchmarking and provide a basis for enhancement activity.

They are also political concepts, in at least two senses. Official statistics provide governments (and to a lesser extent oppositions) with information that enables them to exert influence on systems, or parts of systems. The publication of the first set of UK performance indicators (HEFCE 1999a), for example, led the minister responsible for the sector to express her expectation that those institutions which exhibited poor retention and completion rates would make serious efforts to improve them. Retention and attrition are also politically relevant whenever they enter the more general public arena, particularly where reportage in the press is used to score political points that reflect an editorial standpoint.

However, indexing retention and completion as performance indicators is not as straightforward as casual thinking might suggest, since the publication of indicators is likely to have effects on what is being measured. An institution concerned to improve its performance as regards retention may decide to take the safer option of enrolling only students whose backgrounds point more strongly to student success which, as Bourner et al. (1991: 105) pointed out, could be illiberal, restrictive and discriminatory against those for whom the institutional mission might have signalled a welcome.

Student success

The more that students have to fund themselves through higher education, and the less the level of governmental funding, the weaker is the rationale for using retention and completion as performance indicators. A 'lifelong learning' approach to higher education likewise weakens the rationale for such indicators. Students may choose to dip in and out of higher education as their circumstances permit (which is not unreasonable from their point of view), giving rise to attendance patterns that differ from the full-time, unbroken, expectations of the residential institution.[3] The further students move away from full-time engagement in higher education, the stronger is the case for indexing student success in terms of their 'success per study unit', as is done in Australia.[4] Such an index reflects a student-centred view of higher education and also represents better the success of the partnership between institution and student than do year-based retention and completion statistics (Yorke 1999b).

However one responds to the challenge of indexing student success, the more important point is that a focus on student success implies more clearly the need to give attention to the ways in which an institution can help to facilitate it (Chapters 9 and 10).

The interests of stakeholders

Interest in student retention can be reduced to three stakeholders, students, institutions and the state – as represented by its various agencies, such as the Higher Education Funding Council for England. A review of the interests of these three stakeholders has been explored in more detail elsewhere (Longden 2002b).

Students

Success in higher education brings with it a range of benefits: not only the prospect of rewarding employment (in both senses of 'rewarding'), but the enhancement of cultural and social capital, a commensurate standard of living, and better health than others in the population enjoy. Entrance to the UK labour market without a degree results in a lower financial return than is received by graduates (Johnes and Taylor 1991), and the return has been found to be lower than for those who did not enter higher education in the first place (Blundell et al. 1997). Davies and Elias (2003) show that students who leave higher education without completing a degree programme find it much more difficult than graduates to obtain a 'graduate-level job' or to enter a channel that could be expected to lead to such a job.

Further, the acquisition of a graduate-level job makes it more likely that debts incurred as a student will be paid off relatively quickly and with relative ease. Success, then, is perhaps more important for students than some may recognize at the time when they are thinking about applying to enter higher education. The choice of study programme, and the commitment to it, are critically important.

In a foreword to a report on non-completion in Ireland (Morgan et al. 2001), Don Thornhill, the Chairman of the Republic's Higher Education Authority, reminds both teachers and policy makers not to forget that

> ...for some students who do not complete their courses, the result can be very damaging not just in financial terms – but also in terms of reduced self-esteem and self-confidence.
>
> (Morgan et al. 2001: 6)

Davies and Elias (2003) report the psychological setback felt by some students as a consequence of early withdrawal. For 'MN', it derived from what she perceived others to be thinking about her:

> My family did not talk to me for a long time; they said I'd let them down. They had huge expectations of me; I was the brightest one; the first in the family to go to university
>
> (Davies and Elias 2003: 45)

For 'TL' it was the personal sense of failure, compounded by a sense of loneliness as regards his position:

> I felt I'd failed; having to tell others you have dropped out. I was the only one in the family to go to university so there was no one else to understand why I had done what I'd done.
>
> (Davies and Elias 2003: 45)

Others of Davies and Elias' respondents, though, had felt themselves strengthened by their experience of non-completion. For example, 'SB', whilst observing that telling her parents was the worst thing she had had to do, was able to say:

> I have learned a lot about myself, about people, and about situations, and that experience should be very useful. I have benefited socially, financially and my self-esteem is higher.
>
> (Davies and Elias 2003: 45)

It may be that such students had been able to construe their experience in terms of a learning opportunity rather than as personal inadequacy, or a failure to perform.[5]

The act of engaging in higher education, for most students, is indicative of their commitment. They want to be successful, and some persevere in the face of considerable adversity (examples are mentioned in McGivney (1996) and in Seymour and Hewitt (1997)), perhaps because of factors that are difficult to measure *in situ*,[6] such as motivation (Pintrich 2000), a 'malleable' self-theory (Dweck 1999), self-efficacy (Bandura 1997), and whether the student has a sense of 'belonging' (both academically and socially) in an institution. On the other hand, those who drift into higher education without a strong sense of purpose are likely to exhibit lower levels of commitment and hence persistence: attestations to that effect can be found in the reports by Yorke on research in the UK (1999a, 1999b) and Davies and Elias (2003).

The decision to leave a programme before the end is rarely taken lightly, and is often anguished. In his qualitative study, Longden (2001b) demonstrates that, for some, the departure decision was the culmination of several months of growing doubt, stress and in some cases feelings of depression. The decision once made, there was often a sense of relief. John is quite representative of the cohort that Longden studied following their decision to leave early. Despite John's inability to integrate into the institution either academically or socially, he had not regretted his decision 'to have a go in the first place'. Once he had made his decision, he acknowledged the sense of relief:

> I felt as though it was a huge weight off my shoulders. I really did ... I don't regret it for one minute.
>
> (Longden 2001b: 63)

Institutions

Institutions have a vested interest in their students' success, but student success here is about not only the students obtaining the qualifications for which they have been studying, but also connected with the perceptions of those outside higher education (mainly employers) who will be concerned to ensure that they have recruits who can relatively quickly fulfil the expectations laid upon them. So student success is not only about grade point averages or honours degree classifications but also about the ability to be effective in working with others, solving the 'messy' problems that life throws up, and so on. As Sternberg (1997) would have it, success is dependent on the ability to display both academic and 'practical' intelligence. This points towards the literature on what in the UK is termed 'employability', and the associated issues of teaching, learning, assessment and standards, which are too complex for us to address here.[7]

The extent to which students are successful in attaining qualifications is a primary performance indicator. In the UK, the percentage of graduates gaining employment within six months (or going on to further study) is also published (HEFCE 2002), though the current figures do not differentiate between 'graduate-level jobs' and any jobs. The intention is, though, to refine this indicator in order to reflect the proportion of students who secure graduate-level employment (Rushforth 2003). Our brief discussion of student success in terms of employment acknowledges that employers are stakeholders in students' success – and are particularly strongly so when they support students through higher education programmes.

Retention and completion are important for an institution, since benefit can accrue from positive public perceptions of their success levels. Conversely, an institution with a poor record in this regard is likely to receive adverse publicity, as we illustrate in Chapter 5. Retention may play a part in institutional funding. In England, for example, a full-time student has to persist until the end of the academic year if the institution is to benefit from the 'core' funding that HEFCE attaches to their place.[8] Early withdrawal of students in effect 'wastes' the resources that were committed to recruiting and enrolling them, and the loss may be exacerbated if the charges levied by the institution in respect of tuition are not collected. There is a 'message' here for all institutions, but particularly for those that seek to enrol students from disadvantaged backgrounds: they need to back up their efforts to recruit students with actions that are likely to encourage sustained success.

Departments and programme teams, like institutions as a whole, have an interest in student retention and success. They are judged on a range of student outcomes, both by their external constituencies and by institutional managers (who may use intra- and extra-institutional benchmarking to reach judgements on their effectiveness and efficiency).

A problem for institutions develops where students adopt modes of engagement that are relatively common in the USA – interspersing periods of study with employment or some other kind of commitment. Whilst this may be an ideal resolution of the problem of self-financing through a study programme, such flexibility on the part of the student creates headaches for institutions as regards the prediction of income streams and the provision of resources.

Government

At the beginning of this chapter we outlined the importance of retention and completion to national or state governments, and will not repeat the points here. Aspects of retention and completion that are of governmental significance are explored in respect of South Africa, Australia and England in Chapters 2, 3 and 4 respectively.

Given the legitimate interests of governments, a key role for them is to ensure that relevant research is carried out into matters that bear on retention and completion. The National Center for Educational Statistics (NCES) in the USA, the Department of Education, Science and Training (DEST) in Australia (and its predecessors), the Department for Education and Skills (DfES) (and its forebears) along with HEFCE in the UK have all commissioned or undertaken a substantial amount of useful research. The NCES is a particularly fruitful repository of statistical information, which is freely available on its website.[9]

Where the higher education system is relatively small, such as in the

Republic of Ireland, official bodies such as the Higher Education Authority are able to take a more detailed interest in retention and completion, such as the differential success rates within the system, as broken down by both institution and subject area. The corollary is that they are in a better position to exert leverage directly.

Some matters of importance for governments attract alternative interpretations from researchers. In England, for example, there has been an ongoing concern about student funding, debt, and the implications for non-completion. This is encapsulated in the following quotation from Claire Callender, a prominent researcher on these issues, when she gave evidence to the Education and Employment Select Committee of the House of Commons:

> I think it is fair to say that the DfEE [Department for Education and Employment] perceives student loans to be income and not debt. It only becomes debt when a student leaves university and graduates. The issue is whether such a model of economic rationality reflects the reality of the way students think and behave ... My concern is the extent to which changes in government policy, in terms of student funding, may in some way militate against that overall objective. That is my concern. It is because of the move from grants to loans that students have built up this substantial debt. My concern is about whether worries about debt, and thoughts about debt in advance of going to university, may deter some people. There is then the issue about what role debt plays when students are at university in terms of, for example, dropout.
>
> (House of Commons 2001c: 101, para. 343)

The consequences of commissioning research include the possibility of being faced with findings that are awkward in respect of prevailing public policy – a risk that has to be faced in a democracy.

The costs of non-completion

Non-completion is a cost to the various parties involved in a student's enrolment on a higher education programme. The apportionment of the cost depends, of course, on the structure of funding within the higher education system concerned. The gain to students of participating in higher education for a limited time may well be outweighed by the costs that they (and perhaps their sponsors) have incurred. The institution may not receive its full public funding entitlement if the student does not complete a period of study. The government or funding body is likely to be concerned that the funds it provided for the system have not been used to maximum effect.

In the UK, concern about the cost to public funds of undergraduate non-completion became increasingly important towards the mid–1990s, probably fuelled by the rapid expansion of the higher education sector. The study that was commissioned by the Higher Education Funding Council for England (Yorke et al. 1997) estimated that, for the academic year 1995–96, the cost to the public purse of non-completion in England was approximately £90 million, or around 3 per cent of the funding assigned to the teaching of undergraduate students. At that time, there were three components that contributed to the total cost to public funds – 'core' funding from HEFCE (which was – and still is – formula-based, and caters for student numbers and types of programme); tuition fees; and student maintenance. The changes to the funding methodology that were introduced in 1997 removed the maintenance award from the public commitment and required students to contribute part of their tuition costs.

It is possible to estimate the cost to public finances of student non-continuation, using data available in the public domain. Two possible approaches can be used. The first uses data relating to the funding allocation made by the Government to HEFCE, and narrows this down to the expenditure on undergraduate education. From this figure the estimate of non-completion can be calculated, using non-completion rates. The second approach, used here, is to start from the student numbers enrolled on undergraduate programmes (HESA 2002), the average level of funding for undergraduate students (HEFCE 2003) and the rate of non-continuation (HEFCE 2001a, 2002).

In round numbers this calculation, based on full-time first-degree entrants into English institutions in 1999, gives a total of around £74 million for non-continuation following the first year. This figure is the product of the following:

- £3200 (estimated to be the average unit cost per full-time student across all price groups.
- 230,000 students (approximately) enrolled in English universities and colleges in 1999.
- 0.1 (the proportion of students not continuing from the first to the second year, reflecting the national average of 10 per cent).

When non-continuation between year two and three is factored into the calculation at about 6 per cent, a further £26 million can be added to the cost (this gives credit to students for successfully completed years, and does not treat the whole of their time in higher education as of no benefit). On this basis, the total cost of non-continuation on first-degree programmes is estimated to be, in round figures, about £100 million.

If consideration is then given to sub-degree full-time programmes (which are normally two years in length), it is reasonable to add a further £10 million.

This suggests a total cost to the public finances of around £110 million per year.[10]

Some who seek to make political capital out of the cost of non-completion do their cause no service by exaggeration. One union, in submitting evidence to the Education and Employment Select Committee of the House of Commons (see the context for this in Chapter 4) elected to base its calculation on the gross Funding Council grant of £5 billion and a non-completion rate for full-time undergraduates of 18 per cent, to produce an estimated cost of £900 million (House of Commons 2001c: 139, para. 7). This makes a number of erroneous assumptions, including mistaking the total HEFCE allocation for the amount earmarked for teaching and learning, and ignoring the fact that there are substantial numbers of postgraduate and part-time students to whom the 18 per cent non-completion rate is inapplicable.

Sketches of four higher education systems

In this book we make particular reference to the systems of four countries: Australia, South Africa, the United Kingdom (particularly England), and the United States. In order to provide some background to the contributions from these countries, we briefly sketch the systems that exist in them, readily acknowledging that these sketches can be nothing more than extremely general.

Despite the cultural differences, similar issues can be seen in all of the countries, though the degree to which they are problematic and the precise nature of problems differ from one country to the next. Encouraging under-represented groups into higher education is one consistent theme, whether it be in relation to Hispanics, Native Americans and African Americans in the USA; to non-whites in South Africa; to the Aboriginal and Torres Strait Islander populations in Australia;[11] or to lower socio-economic groups and some ethnic minorities in the UK. Associated with the issue of participation is that of retention, which presents challenges whatever the nature of the disadvantaged group.

A second concern is that of student funding, especially in respect of those deemed to be particularly in need of support. A third is the differentiation in rates of retention and student success across different groups in higher education, and between different types of institution. For example, retention of disadvantaged students continues to challenge leaders in the US higher education system, particularly where African American students attend predominantly white colleges and universities. About 80 per cent of African American students attend predominantly white institutions, yet their success levels are disproportionately low. Love (1993) suggests that the causes of low success rates include financial and academic problems, isolation and alienation.

Australia

Australia's first university opened in Sydney in 1850, which led to each of the six states establishing its own university and to the establishment of the Australian National University in Canberra. After the Second World War, student numbers rapidly increased, with new universities being created in order to cater for the demand. By 1987 the higher education system was educating a total of nearly 400,000 students in 19 universities and 46 colleges of advanced education (CAEs). A significant policy change was introduced in 1989 with the creation of the Unified National System of higher education (UNS), which involved the incorporation of many of the CAEs into existing universities as well as the amalgamation of other CAEs to form new universities.

Australia currently has 39 publicly funded institutions and a further five private institutions, four of which receive limited public funding, which provide education for well over 700,000 students (DEST 2003), with international students comprising about 15 per cent of this student population.

The creation of the UNS was accompanied by a fundamental change to the financing of students' study. The Higher Education Contribution Scheme (HECS) required home students to make a contribution towards their university education through payments, either deferred until their post-graduation income reached a threshold figure or paid 'up front' at a discount. At the same time international students lost the subsidy that they had enjoyed up to then. Since its introduction, HECS and the fees charged to overseas students have undergone changes as the government has implemented its policy of cutting public expenditure (Gamage and Mininberg 2003: 191). In 2003 the government proposed that universities would have the freedom to vary the HECS contributions to a maximum of 30 per cent above the standard rate for particular fields of study. As Gamage and Mininberg (2003: 191) note, the developments relating to HECS have already increased the burden on individual students during the period of study and subsequently, because of the accumulation of debt.

The changes to HECS threaten the participation of under-represented groups, which has for a decade been a facet of the government's equity policy. The performance indicators for indigenous populations show a lower uptake and in some cases poorer retention rate, despite over a decade of implementation. With students increasingly undertaking part-time employment to help them to pay their way through university (James 2000; McInnis, James et al. 2000), there are threats to student engagement, retention and completion.

South Africa

South African higher education exists in a political and social context which has undergone a rapid and massive transformation from apartheid to democracy. In 1996 a governmental White Paper set out what had to be done:

> The challenge is to redress past inequalities and to transform the higher education system to serve a new social order, to meet pressing national needs, and to respond to new realities and opportunities.
>
> (National Commission on Higher Education 1996: 7)

The aim has been to promote equity of access and a fair chance of success for all who seek to realize their potential through higher education. The problem is that, as Eckel (2001: 109) says, South African institutions do not have the 'luxury of time to implement transformational changes ... stakes are high and the consequences of failure serious'. Bunting sets out, in Chapter 2, the shape of the evolving higher education system in South Africa and shows the magnitude of the challenge that the system faces.

United Kingdom

Higher education in the UK expanded from the elite system which had existed until the first half of the twentieth century (when the participation rate for school leavers was less than 10 per cent), there being two main sources of impetus: the Robbins Report (Committee on Higher Education 1963) which led to the creation of a number of what were seen at that time as 'new universities', and the decision of the Conservative administration of the late 1980s to allow significant further expansion.[12] The Open University, created by the Labour government of 1964–70, opened up part-time education to many more people than had been accommodated in the higher education system of the time. A 'binary divide' between universities and what was at the time termed 'the public sector of higher education' existed until 1992, with the latter being funded to a significant extent through local education authorities. The 'Education Reform Act' of 1992 established a unified system, with public funding for institutions being channelled through national funding councils in England, Scotland and Wales and through the erstwhile Department of Education in Northern Ireland (DENI).

Following the process of devolution, which began to take shape in 1998, responsibility for higher education became divided between the DfES in England, the Scottish Parliament, the Welsh Assembly and what has latterly become the Department for Employment and Learning (DEL) in Northern Ireland. In the first three of these national systems, funding for institutions continues to be channelled through the respective national funding councils.

The expansion has been followed by a realization that the state could not continue to bear as much of the funding burden as had hitherto been the case, and the way in which this was approached in the mid-1990s is outlined in Chapter 4. Here we merely note that the funding of institutions through tuition fees and the provision of student support (jointly, an electorally sensitive issue) have been approached in different ways in different parts of the UK.[13]

There has also been a strong concern to increase the representation in higher education from traditionally disadvantaged groups – particularly lower socio-economic groups, whose level of engagement has remained low despite attempts to encourage it to rise. There is a recognition that the roots of the problem lie much further back, in children's school years, and there have been various efforts to exert influence on children at that time: the results cannot be expected to appear quickly.

The United States of America

Higher education in the USA can be traced back to the establishment of Harvard University in 1638. Initially the universities in the USA were established along the elitist lines of those in the UK, but higher education became 'massified' relatively early, particular influences being the 'GI Bill' of 1944, the boost given to education in the 1960s by the Russian launching of Sputnik 1, and the introduction of Pell grants and loans in 1972. In outlining developments, Keohane (1999) notes that the benefit of a university education was seen in terms of upward mobility and, by extension, about an improved quality and standard of life experience.[14]

There are in excess of 3700 institutions which accommodate around 60 per cent of 18-year-olds.[15] Institutional provision ranges from small private denominational colleges of fewer than 1000 students to large state universities with over 50,000 on-campus students. The types of institution include major research institutions with teaching, large state-sponsored comprehensive universities, highly selective private liberal arts universities, community colleges and the recently developed 'for profit' institutions such as the University of Phoenix. Hence generalization about American higher education provision is problematic.

Higher education is the province of the separate states rather than the federal government, which 'plays a fairly circumscribed role, focusing mainly on student aid and federal research monies' (Eckel 2001: 106). The states monitor institutional performance using indicators (inter-state and intra-state comparisons being important[16]), with some states coupling performance to funding mechanisms.[17] Retention and success rates have been important measures of performance of state higher education systems and, as Braxton (2000b) notes, have posed a long-standing problem to colleges and universities across the USA.

2

Student retention: a macro perspective from South Africa

Ian A. Bunting

Overview

This chapter offers an account, from a system-level perspective, of student retention in South Africa's higher education system. It begins with an account of the flows of students into and out of the public higher education system. It then discusses the main retention problems experienced by the South African higher education system. The chapter ends with a brief account of new national policies and plans, whose implementation should have an impact on the problems of student output and retention rates raised in this chapter.

Higher education in South Africa

South Africa's higher education system is primarily a public one. A small private sector exists, but most of that sector's students have joint registrations, through partnership agreements, with institutions in the public higher education system. Less than 1 per cent of South Africa's higher education students are registered solely for academic programmes offered by private higher education institutions.

A binary divide exists at present in the public higher education system. South Africa's public higher education institutions were divided in 2001 into a group of 21 universities and 15 technikons. In 2002 two of the technikons merged to form a new, larger institution. The technikons are institutions which offer primarily vocationally directed qualifications in applied disciplines. In the 2001 academic year, 48 per cent of technikon students were following programmes in the fields of business and management and 32 per cent programmes in applied science and technology. The remaining 20 per cent were following programmes in applied humanities. The technikons do not offer general formative or professional academic programmes of the kind found in the universities, and are not as active in research as the universities. (See Bunting (1994) for a discussion of the differences between universities and technikons.)

In the 2001 academic year, South Africa's public universities and technikons registered a head count total of 645,000 students. This head count total generated a full-time equivalent enrolled student total of 430,000.

Some of the key features of the 2001 head count enrolment total of 645,000 students are these:

- 610,000 (or 95 per cent) of enrolled students in 2001 were either South African citizens or foreign citizens with permanent residence rights in South Africa. About 30,000 students from other African countries were studying in South Africa on temporary entrance permits. The remaining 5000 were mainly from Europe and the USA.
- 59 per cent of these 645,000 students were registered for 'contact' or on-campus academic programmes, and the remaining 41 per cent were registered for 'distance' or off-campus programmes.
- 428,000 students (66 per cent of the total) were enrolled in universities and 217,000 (34 per cent) in technikons.

Most higher education students in South Africa follow undergraduate programmes. In 2001, 385,000 (60 per cent of the total) were enrolled for three-year undergraduate degrees and diplomas; 143,000 (22 per cent) for undergraduate degrees of four years or longer; 40,000 (6 per cent) for masters or doctoral programmes; and 55,000 (9 per cent) for other post-graduate qualifications below the level of masters. The remaining 22,000 (3 per cent) were enrolled for formal courses but not for a specific qualification (they were what are described as 'occasional' or 'non-degree' students).

> Female and black students had the major shares of the enrolment total of 645,000 students. In 2001 52% of all students in public universities and technikons were female and 72% were black.
>
> (Department of Education 2001c)

The gross participation rate in public higher education in South Africa in 2001 was 16 per cent, calculated by dividing the enrolment total of 610,000 students who are South African citizens by the total of South Africa's population in the 20–24 year age group. This participation rate is low because of problems with both inflows into the higher education system and student retention (see later).

At least 95 per cent of the students entering the South African public higher education system come from the country's school system. The annual outflow from this school system is summed up in broad terms in the Figure 2.1 below. This figure does not represent any specific year. It indicates what the typical outflow from the school system has been over the past three years.

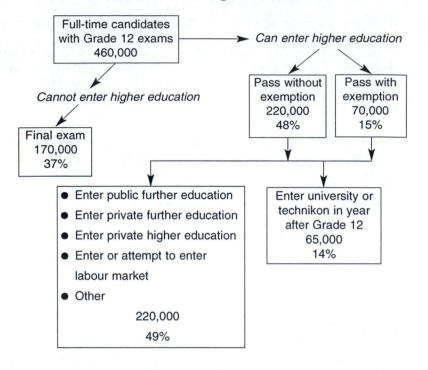

Figure 2.1 Annual outflow from South African school system (Source: adapted from Bunting 2002c)

Figure 2.1 shows that of the approximately 460,000 pupils who each year write the final national school examinations, about 290,000 qualify for entry to a public university or technikon. However, because a two-tier school exit system remains in place, 220,000 of those who pass the final school examinations do not obtain matriculation exemption and so cannot enter degree-level studies. They are able to enter only undergraduate diploma-level studies, primarily at a technikon. The diagram shows also that only 15 per cent of those who write the final school examination obtain matriculation exemption and as a result qualify for entry to degree-level studies at a university or technikon. The diagram shows finally that 65,000 (or 14 per cent) of those who write the final school examination enter a public university or technikon in the year immediately after leaving school.

The annual intake into the South African higher education system includes these 65,000 'straight-from-school students' plus a further 65,000 first-time entering undergraduates (defined as students who had not previously been registered at any higher education institution) who had left school in some earlier years. Students in this first-time entering undergraduate category represent about 20 per cent of the total public higher education enrolment in South Africa in any given year. The numbers in

other entry categories are lower: transfer undergraduates (that is, undergraduates moving between institutions) have only a 6 per cent share of the
total public higher education enrolment in any given year, and new postgraduates (that is, students entering postgraduate studies for the first-time)
normally have only a 5 per cent share. These new postgraduates could
include students who completed a first qualification the previous year.

Figure 2.2 below offers a summary, based on data for 1999–2001, of
annual outflows from the South African public higher education system.

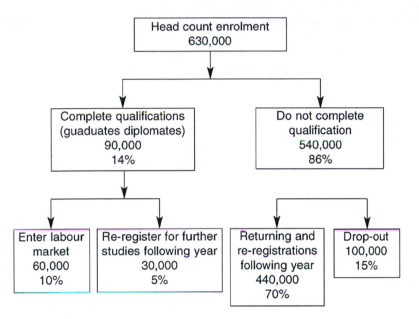

Figure 2.2   Annual outflows from South African public universities and technikons
(Source: adapted from Bunting 2001a)

The data for these years show that the higher education system has typically
been able to retain into the following year only about 75 per cent of its
students. The majority of those who do not return in the following year
(100,000 or 15 per cent of the total annual enrolment) are students who
have dropped out of the system without completing a formal qualification.
Only about 90,000 students (or 14 per cent of the total annual enrolment)
complete their qualifications, and only about 60,000 of these enter the
South African labour market each year.

Student retention and the apartheid context

Any analysis of student retention in South Africa's public higher education
system has to take account of the apartheid context from which this system

emerged. During the apartheid years, South Africa's public universities and technikons were placed into race-based categories. Seventeen of these institutions (not including the two dedicated distance institutions) had been established by the apartheid government to 'serve the interests of the white population group', and 13 to 'serve the interests of the African population group'. Two of the remaining were set up to 'serve the interests of the coloured population group', and the remaining two to 'serve the interests of the Indian population group' (see Bunting 2002b for a more detailed account of these apartheid categories). For most analytical and descriptive purposes these institutions have in recent years been divided into five groups: a group of ten historically white universities, a group of ten historically black universities, a group of seven historically white technikons, a group of seven historically black technikons, and finally a group consisting of the two dedicated distance institutions. The total number of public technikons was reduced to 14 in April 2002, when M.L. Sultan Technikon (an historically black technikon) merged with Natal Technikon (an historically white technikon) to form the new Durban Institute of Technology.

The data available show that there have been notable differences between the performances of these groupings of public higher education institutions, as far as student inflows and outflows are concerned. For example, the historically white universities have had lower dropout rates than the historically black universities. Universities in this group have furthermore been able to encourage higher proportions of first-degree qualifiers to return for postgraduate studies than have the historically black universities. On average about 85 per cent of all students registered at historically white universities in a particular year have returned in the following year either to continue their studies or to start a new postgraduate programme. The comparable proportion for historically black universities is only 75 per cent, and for both groupings of technikons is only 70 per cent. These proportions are clear indications that their student retention rates are significantly different from those of the historically white universities.

The racial composition of the different groupings of institutions is a major element in the differences in retention performance. In the current South African context, white students continue to be more privileged than the majority of black students, in terms of both educational and socio-economic background. In recent years, however, institutions that have large proportions of white students have tended also to be those in which black students from the new South African elite are enrolled.

In 2001, 55 per cent of all students in contact or on-campus programmes in the historically white universities were white, compared to proportions of less than 2 per cent for the historically black universities. This has led to the historically white universities having higher levels of student retention and lower levels of student dropout than the historically black institutions.

The situation as far as the historically white technikons are concerned is an anomalous one. In 2001 about 25 per cent of their students were white, which implies that they were, like the historically white universities, attracting more advantaged students than their historically black counter-parts, which have enrolments of less than 2 per cent of white students. The evidence available shows, however, that the performance of the historically white technikons, as far as student retention and dropouts are concerned, is probably worse than that of the historically black technikons.

Dropout and cohort completion rates in South African public higher education

The two central problems of student retention in the South African public higher education system have been flagged in the previous two sections. Table 2.1 shows that the rate of retention, measured as the proportion of students registered in year n who do not complete a qualification and who re-register in year n+1, is 70 per cent (the proportion of re-registrations including returning graduates is 75 per cent). This proportion of 70 per cent, which appears to be a reasonable one, hides the problems of high dropout and low completion rates in the system.

The data available suggest that each year about 100,000 students registered in the public higher education system drop out without having completed a degree or diploma. This is equivalent to a loss of about 15 per cent of the annual head count total. The data also indicate that only about 90,000 graduates/diplomates are produced each year by the public higher education system. This total amounts to about 14 per cent of the annual total of students enrolled in the system. In its *National Plan for Higher Education*, the Ministry of Education states that these proportions of students dropping out and graduating are unacceptable ones, which '... represent a huge wastage of resources, both human and financial ... (and which) are likely to be an impediment in achieving the economic development goals of the Government' (Department of Education 2001a: 21).

In reaching this judgement about the high levels of wastage in public higher education, the Ministry has not been able to use system-wide long-itudinal studies of the performance of cohorts of students. There are two reasons for this:

- Very few universities and technikons in South Africa have undertaken such cohort studies, either at the request of government or on their own initiative, and
- The national higher education management information system has only since the 2000 academic year contained the student unit record data which make national cohort studies possible.

The Ministry has as a consequence been forced to find sets of indicators which can serve as proxies for standard cohort studies. The indicators adopted as proxies have been simple ones. They have been 'graduation

rates', defined as the number of students graduating with a specific qualification in a given year divided by the number of students registered for that
qualification in that same year. (See Bunting 2001b for a more detailed
discussion of graduation rates as proxies for cohort flow.)

The data averages in Table 2.1 offer examples of graduation rates for
certain typical qualifications. These averages were derived by dividing the
total of graduates for 1999–2001 by the corresponding head count enrolment totals for these three years.

Table 2.1 Graduates/diplomates as proportions of enrolments: averages for 1999–
2001

	3-year undergraduate degrees & diplomas	Masters degrees	Doctoral degrees
Historically white universities	18%	20%	12%
Historically black universities	13%	11%	9%
AVERAGE	**16%**	**19%**	**12%**
Historically white technikons	13%	10%	See note
Historically black technikons	15%	6%	See note
AVERAGE	**14%**	**9%**	See note

Source: Department of Education (2001c). Data for universities are for degrees only, and for
technikons are for diplomas only. The institutions listed do not include the dedicated distance
education institutions: University of South Africa and Technikon South Africa.
Note: The numbers in these cells are too small for percentages to be meaningful.

The proportions in this table can be converted, using flow models based on
empirical data on enrolment growth and dropouts, to cohort completion
rates. These flow models show, for example, that with three-year undergraduate qualifications in a context of stable enrolment totals and low
dropout rates (10 per cent at the end of year one and 5 per cent at the end
of other years), if the ratio of graduates to enrolments in any academic year
is at least 25 per cent, then the cohort completion rate will be at least 75 per
cent. What this cohort completion rate of 75 per cent means is that if (say)
1000 first-time entering undergraduates enter a three-year undergraduate
qualification, then 750 of them will, by the end of a five-year period, have
completed all the requirements of their qualification. These flow models
show, also in the context of three-year undergraduate qualifications with
stable enrolment totals, that if the ratio of graduates to enrolments in any
academic year is 20 per cent, then the cohort completion rate will be only
60 per cent. If the ratio of graduates to enrolments is only 15 per cent, then
the cohort completion rate would be 45 per cent.

Similar flow models can be constructed for masters and doctoral degrees.
These show that if the ratio of masters graduates to masters enrolments in
any academic year is 33 per cent, then the cohort completion rate will be at
least 80 per cent. However if the ratio of masters graduates to masters
enrolments in any academic year is only 20 per cent, then the cohort

completion rate will probably be 50 per cent. If the ratio of doctoral graduates to doctoral enrolments in any academic year is (say) 20 per cent, then the cohort completion rate will probably be 75 per cent. If this ratio of doctoral graduates to doctoral enrolments in any academic year falls to 15 per cent, then the cohort completion rate will probably be only 55 per cent.

These flow models and the average ratios of graduates to enrolments permit a table of estimated cohort completion rates to be calculated. These are set out in Table 2.2 below:

Table 2.2 Estimates of cohort completion rates: based on data for 1999–2001

	3-year undergraduate qualifications	Masters degrees	Doctoral degrees
Historically white universities	55%	50%	45%
Historically black universities	40%	25%	35%
AVERAGE	**50%**	**50%**	**45%**
Historically white technikons	40%	25%	See note
Historically black technikons	45%	15%	See note
AVERAGE	**42%**	**20%**	See note

Source: Bunting 2001
Note: The numbers in these cells are too small for percentages to be meaningful.

As was stated earlier, the view of the national Ministry of Education is that the levels of student wastage reflected in Table 2.2 are exceptionally and unacceptably high. Table 2.3 below illustrates this point in relation to undergraduate qualifications. It shows (a) what the average annual intakes

Table 2.3 First-time entering undergraduate cohort totals and expected totals of graduates

	Average annual intake of new undergraduate students	Total expected to complete qualification after 6 years of study	Completion rate of cohort
Historically white universities	35,000	19,000	55%
Historically black universities	25,000	10,000	40%
Historically white technikons	30,000	12,000	40%
Historically black technikons	15 000	7,000	45%
Total	**105,000**	**48,000**	**45%**

Notes
Source: Data derived from student statistics tables published by the Department of Education between 1999 and 2001. The calculations in this table assume that the completion rate for all undergraduate qualifications will be the same as that for 3-year qualifications. The institutions listed do not include the dedicated distance education institutions: University of South Africa and Technikon South Africa.

of first-time entering undergraduate students are into the universities and technikons listed in Table 2.2 above, and (b) how many of each of these entering cohorts are likely to complete, under current circumstances, their qualifications.

The data in the table above highlight these concerns in a stark manner. As many as 57,000 of the approximately 105,000 new undergraduates entering the contact or residential universities and technikons each year will drop out without completing their qualifications. Only 48,000 will be retained until the successful completion of their studies (which could be for as long as six years).

The retention problems with masters and doctoral students are equally serious. The historically white universities recruit a large majority of South Africa's masters and doctoral students (in 2001, 70 per cent of all masters students and 85 per cent of all doctoral students). The data show that at these historically white universities (a) only 50 out of every 100 students entering masters degree studies eventually graduate, and (b) only 45 out of every 100 students entering doctoral degree studies eventually graduate.

Causes of student retention problems in South Africa

The retention problems, and in particular the high dropout and low cohort completion rates discussed in earlier sections, can be ascribed to a number of different causes. These include problems with the national public school system and its inability to produce sufficient numbers of school-leavers with the knowledge and skills required for the successful completion of higher education studies. They include also problems with the academic programme offerings and the teaching methods of most higher education institutions. These have not been changed quickly enough to meet the needs of a new, transformed public higher education system.

Two other more specific higher education-related problems are these:

1. Many of those from disadvantaged backgrounds are unable to meet the high private costs of higher education, and drop out for financial reasons.
2. The application and admission procedures employed by many institutions are inadequate and lead to students entering academic programmes for which they are not suited and about which they have little or no prior knowledge.

Private costs of higher education

At the beginning of 1980s the funding of South Africa's historically white universities was based on the principle that, since higher education generates both public and private benefits, its costs must be shared by the government and by individual students. During the 1980s and early 1990s, this principle was extended to the historically black universities and to all technikons. The result has been that by 2001 government appropriations accounted for only 47 per cent of the total income of public universities and technikons in South Africa. Tuition fees charged to students amounted to 22 per cent, with the balance of 31 per cent coming from private sources such as the residence fees paid by students, private grants and contracts and investment income (Department of Education 1982, 2002b).

The phrase 'tuition fees charged to students' was used deliberately in the paragraph above. In 2001 public higher education institutions in South Africa sent tuition fee bills to students and/or their families totalling R3500 million (the exchange rates in 2001 were approximately R10 to a US dollar, and approximately R16 to a pound sterling). Public institutions, when sending out these bills, knew that the experience of the past few years would be repeated: at least 15 per cent (or R525 million) of the tuition fees charged to students would not be paid in 2001, and the major proportion of unpaid tuition fees would be those charged by the historically black institutions.

The relationship between these charges for tuition fees and other sources of income can be seen in Table 2.4 below.

Table 2.4 Sources of income of public universities and technikons in 2001 (Rand millions) (Adapted from Bunting 2002a)

	Appropriation	Tuition fees	Income	Total
Historically white universities	3200	1350	2900	7450
Historically black universities	1600	700	1100	3400
Historically white technikons	1200	500	450	2150
Historically black technikons	700	250	200	1150
Distance institutions	1000	650	350	2000
Total	**7700**	**3450**	**5000**	**16,150**

What this table does not show is that tuition fees are not the only fees charged to students. Students who live in halls of residence run by public higher education institutions (approximately 20 per cent of contact or on-campus students) are expected to pay housing and catering fees which amount to about double an average tuition fee. In 2001 tuition fees charged by universities and technikons were on average about R8000 per full-time equivalent enrolled student, and residence fees (for housing plus all meals) were on average about R16,000 per student. These residence fees are included in the fee bills sent to students, and large proportions of these would in any year remain uncollected.

The data in Table 2.4 indicate clearly what effects unpaid tuition and residence fees are likely to have on the public higher education system.

The impact of unpaid fees, as was stated earlier, has been experienced primarily by historically black institutions. The historically black universities in particular have in recent years experienced serious cash flow problems because of unpaid student fees. They have had to deal with cash shortage problems by taking out short-term loans in the form of overdrafts from commercial banks. To cover these overdrafts, institutions have had to put pressure on students to pay outstanding fees. The main step taken has been that of refusing to re-register, at the start of an academic year, any student who had either tuition or residence fees outstanding from the previous year. Because few students and their families have been able to pay outstanding fees, the main consequence of the pressure on students to pay has been sharp increases in dropout rates.

Those refused permission to re-register because of outstanding fee debts are described colloquially in South Africa as 'financial exclusions'.

Application and admission procedures

South Africa does not at present have either a central information service for potential applicants to the public higher education system or a national 'clearing house' for actual applicants. Each public higher education institution is expected to market is own academic programmes to potential applicants and to operate its own applications and admissions service.

Institutional performance in this regard has been patchy. For example, most historically white universities have been able to market their academic programmes reasonably successfully in the media as well as through direct contacts with their key feeder schools. These institutions would normally receive about two applications for every new entry place available, and would as a result be able both to select a cohort of new undergraduate students from a large pool of applicants and to complete selection procedures for their new intakes some weeks before the start of a new academic year.

Many historically black institutions, in marked contrast, have not been able to market their academic programmes in the same ways as historically white universities. This, when linked to their overall financial problems, has meant that they have not been able to operate applications and admissions offices which are as large and as efficient as those at historically white institutions. Historically black institutions, as a consequence of this, have had difficulty in filling their available places for new undergraduate entrants in advance of the start of an academic year. They have had to rely on what are described as 'walk-in' registrations to fill their places. These 'walk-ins' tend to be school-leavers who have not applied in advance for a higher education place, and who arrive at an institution on registration day without having received either prior guidance or advance information on what studies at that institution entail. Some historically black institutions have reported that about 80 per cent of their new undergraduate registrations in any academic year are 'walk-ins', who have to be placed in whatever academic programmes have places available. Their defence of this 'walk-in' system has been that if these very late applicants were not enrolled, then institutions' overall financial situation would be even shakier than it is now. Declines in student enrolments impact critically on the financial positions of institutions, since government subsidies, under the formulas currently in place, are generated primarily by student enrolments.

Institutions which make use of a large scale of 'walk-in' registrations experience, not unexpectedly, high levels of student dropout at the end of the first year of study. In a number of institutions up to 40 per cent of new undergraduates drop out by the end of their first year of study.

New national policies and plans

The South African government has recognized that many of the problems discussed in previous sections of this paper flow from the apartheid origins of the public higher education system. The government of national unity, which came into office after the first democratic elections in South Africa, set up in 1995 a national commission which was given the brief of developing a policy framework for the transformation of higher education in South Africa. This commission reported in 1996 (National Commission on Higher Education 1996), and those of the proposals accepted by the government were published in 1997 in a White Paper entitled *A Programme for the Transformation of Higher Education* (Department of Education 1997).

The 1997 White Paper set out a policy framework containing goals, values and principles which were intended to lead to a higher education system which would:

> ... promote equity of access and fair chances of success to all seeking to realise their potential through higher education ... meet, through well-planned and co-ordinated, teaching, learning and research programmes, national development needs, including ... high-skilled employment needs ... support a democratic ethos and a culture of human rights ... contribute to the advancement of all forms of knowledge and scholarship ...
>
> (Department of Education 1997: 1.14)

These goals were consolidated in a national implementation plan which the Ministry of Education published at the beginning of 2001 (Department of Education 2001a). The aspects of this national plan which have a direct impact on the problems of student retention discussed earlier in this paper include proposals to:

- Restructure the public higher education landscape in order to overcome the apartheid-induced fragmentation and inefficiencies of the current system;

- Use a national planning system linked to the government funding of institutions as the main steering mechanism for the restructured system; and
- Establish a national higher education information and applications service.

The final section of this chapter deals with the first two proposals; the third is currently under consideration by the Ministry.

Restructuring the higher education system

The government takes the restructuring of the public higher education system to be a key transformation task. A national working group was therefore appointed in April 2001 to advise the Minister of Education on appropriate arrangements for consolidating the provision of public higher education in South Africa, in ways which would help it shake off the problems of its apartheid origins. This working group was specifically requested to formulate proposals on the ways in which the number of public universities and technikons could be reduced from the 2001 total of 36. The working group's report was completed at the end of 2001, and was released at the beginning of 2002 (Department of Education 2001b).

The government accepted most of the proposals of the working group and published in May 2002 its intention to reduce, primarily through merger processes, the number of public higher education institutions to 21. Comments on the proposals were invited from the institutions involved in the proposed mergers and from other interested parties. These comments were reviewed by the Ministry in November 2002, and a new set of proposals was submitted to, and approved by, the national cabinet in December 2002.

It is now the intention of government to reduce, over the next three years, the 2001 totals of 21 public universities and 15 public technikons to the following:

- eleven contact universities, with a combined enrolment total of about 222,000 students;
- five contact technikons, with a combined enrolment total of about 122,000 students;
- three contact 'comprehensive institutions' formed through the merging of universities and technikons, with a combined enrolment total of about 85,000 students;
- two contact 'comprehensive institutions' formed through the inclusion of technikon programmes in two current universities, with a combined enrolment total of about 12,000; and
- one dedicated distance 'comprehensive institution' formed through the merging of the current distance university and the current distance technikon, with a combined enrolment total of about 205,000 students.

This process will involve eight major mergers, and at least nine incorporations of satellite campuses into different institutions.

The effect which this restructuring is expected to have on student retention and dropout problems is summed up in these comments made by the government on its first set of 2002 merger proposals:

> The proposals for the restructuring and consolidation of the institutional landscape ... will enable the necessary structural changes to be effected, which will lay the foundation for the transformation and reconstruction of the higher education system. However, institutional restructuring is not in itself sufficient to achieve the broader goals and objectives for the transformation and reconstruction of the higher education system ... It would, however, lay the basis for creating a strong institution through, for instance:

> - Ensuring better staff: student ratios thus enabling the development of strategies to improve poor throughput and graduation rates.
> - Rationalisation of programmes where there is duplication and overlap, which would allow for a more effective and efficient distribution of programmes...
>
> (Department of Education 2002c: 1–2)

This restructuring of the higher education landscape will be a long, difficult process. Because of the disruptive effects which any merger process could have on the institutions involved, improvements in their efficiency may only be realized over a period of some years. In these institutions, in other words, problems of student retention may well continue, if not become worse.

The Ministry of Education has, however, decided that it cannot simply sit back and wait for the merger processes to be completed before taking steps designed to improve the student outputs of the higher education system. It will use the steering mechanisms discussed below to move the public higher education system towards higher levels of student output efficiency.

Planning and funding in the higher education system

A new government funding framework, based on a planning-steering model of national higher education governance, has been under discussion for some years and is likely to be implemented in the 2004 academic year.[18] Under the new framework, the government will not adopt the 'hands-off' approach built into existing funding formulas. It will use instead planning and funding mechanisms to steer the higher education system towards the realization of national goals. Since the primary functions of the public higher education system are teaching and research, government will in future fund institutions to produce knowledge outputs in the form of graduates and research findings.

The government's starting point for its annual higher education budget will therefore not be, as is the case with the present formulas in use in South Africa, a calculation of actual costs in the higher education system. It will decide first of all what it can afford to spend on higher education, and then will allocate funds to institutions in accordance with national development priorities. Under the new funding framework, the allocation of government funds to individual higher education institutions will become a top-down process of the kind set out in Figure 2.3 below.

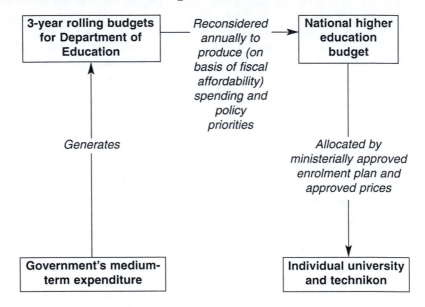

Figure 2.3   Determing and distributing the national higher education budget

A crucial aspect of this new framework is that the allocation of funds to public higher education institutions will depend, not on their actual costs, but rather on a plan which is approved by the Ministry and which takes their institutional performance into account.

Improving the completion rates of cohorts of students is a key example of an aspect of institutional performance which will be taken into account in determining the numbers of funded student places to be assigned to institutions. In its 2001 National Plan, the Ministry says this:

> The Ministry expects all institutions to prioritise and focus their efforts in the next five years on improving the efficiency of the outputs from the system based on ... benchmarks for graduation rates ... The benchmarks have been calculated by reviewing student cohort models, involving a combination of retention rates, dropout rates and graduation rates over a five-year period. They have been developed taking into account South African conditions, which include current performance

and the fact that a large number of under prepared students enter higher education.

(Department of Education 2001a: 23)

The benchmarks set out in the National Plan are based on expectations that the completion rate of any cohort of students entering any programme of undergraduate or postgraduate studies in a South African university or technikon should be at least 75 per cent. The funding incentive for an institution to move towards these benchmarks will be that its number of student places approved for funding could in future be reduced if it is not able to demonstrate that it is making significant moves towards the achievement of these benchmarks.

Other funding incentives will be based on other principles in the new framework. One of these principles is that since government provides funds for higher education institutions for the delivery of services which are in the national interest, teaching outputs will be funded. These funded outputs will be the graduates and diplomates who have completed all the requirements of their qualifications.

In terms of the new funding framework, institutions which improve student retention and output rates can expect a double financial reward:

1. Continuation of, or even increases in, their numbers of funded student numbers; and
2. Direct financial rewards for the numbers of graduates/diplomates produced.

3

Access and retention in Australian higher education

Craig McInnis and Richard James

Overview

Many more people from all sections of society commence higher education in Australia than did so 15 years ago. Yet higher education is still not equally attainable for all Australians, nor seen as equally relevant by all Australians. Two broad conclusions can be stated about the changing patterns of participation in Australian higher education. First, participation increased considerably during the late 1980s and early 1990s, before the rate of expansion levelled off in the late 1990s. Second, though there have been major gains in access for most identified equity target groups, some groups remain seriously under-represented in participation share, in particular people from lower socio-economic backgrounds, people from rural and isolated areas, and indigenous people. Getting students to university is one thing, keeping them is another. A great deal of energy and resources in Australian universities is now targeted at retaining students, especially those whose social and educational background put them at risk of early departure. In this chapter we provide an outline of developments in policy and practice aimed at improving levels of participation and a review of recent research and programmes concerned with retaining students.

A period of expansion, 1987–2002

Participation in higher education in Australia expanded dramatically soon after the creation in 1987 of a Unified National System of Higher Education. In 1987 there were 394,000 university students (DETYA 2000), by 2001 the number of students had swelled to over 726,000 including both domestic and international students (DEST 2002b) with a levelling off in the growth rate evident only in the past three or four years.

Recent estimates suggest 90 per cent of each age cohort can be expected to enter tertiary education at some stage, with roughly equal numbers participating in higher education and vocational education and training (and with many people undertaking various combinations of both) (Aungles et al. 2000). The lifetime probability of entering higher education of the 1995 age cohort was estimated to be 45 per cent, placing Australia among the top-ranking OECD countries in terms of access. Of the 45 per cent of each age cohort anticipated to enter higher education, two-thirds are likely to do so immediately after school and the remaining one-third will do so as mature-age students (Aungles et al. 2000).

Typically, around 70 per cent of students enrol full-time, close to 20 per cent enrol part-time, and a little over 10 per cent are external students (Dobson 2001). Two-thirds of part-time students are mature-age students. Since the expansion of the higher education system following the Second World War, Australia has had a tradition of adult participation in higher education. In some universities over half the students are aged 25 years or more, and the share of students aged 30 years or more hovered between 26 and 28 per cent throughout the 1990s.

The expansion of access during the 1990s was encouraged by innovative student fee arrangements. Australia has a predominantly public university system, with 39 public universities. Undergraduate students contribute to the cost of their education through a deferred payment scheme, the Higher Education Contribution Scheme (HECS), managed by the federal government. HECS was conceived as a way of funding the expansion of the system while at the same time reducing income barriers to enrolment and the pressure on students to undertake paid employment while studying. HECS has generally been perceived to be a fair system. Universities are also allowed to enrol domestic undergraduate students on a full-fee basis, within certain regulatory constraints, but only 3 per cent of students are enrolled in this manner (DEST 2002a). At the time of writing, a major national review of higher education has recommended new funding arrangements, including a further deregulation of student fees. The proposal, likely to face strong opposition in parliament, would give universities discretion in setting the Higher Education Contribution Scheme rate for individual courses, allowing charges up to 30 per cent above the standard Commonwealth schedule with the exception of courses in the national priority fields of teaching and nursing (Nelson 2002; DEST 2003).

Efforts to widen access

Despite the expansion of participation, policies for widening access have had mixed success and there remains a significant social stratification in higher education participation. The objective of equity of access became firmly embedded in federal policy for higher education following the landmark report *A Fair Chance for All* (DEET 1990). This report highlighted the persistent under-representation in Australian higher education of six population groups (see, for instance, Anderson and Vervoorn 1983) later to become equity target groups. These people were people from lower socio-economic backgrounds, rural and isolated people, Aboriginal and Torres Strait Islanders, people with disabilities, people from non-English-speaking backgrounds, and women in five fields designated as non-traditional areas of study. Since 1987, universities have been required to provide the government with annual equity plans outlining strategies for improving the access, participation, success and retention of these designated groups.

During this period much progress has been made, yet there remain unresolved equity issues. The participation of women has improved substantially. Around 55 per cent of commencing undergraduates are now female, slightly above their population share of 52 per cent. Aungles et al. (2000) estimate that the lifetime probability of females entering higher education is 52.5 per cent, compared with 38.1 per cent for males. However, women are over-represented in the fields of education and health and remain under-represented in engineering. They also remain under-represented in some areas of postgraduate education, most notably in doctoral programmes. Higher education has also been successful in attracting people from non-English-speaking backgrounds, highlighting the high educational aspirations and achievements of many immigrant communities. Students from non-English-speaking backgrounds were slightly over-represented on population share during the 1990s. The participation share has dropped in recent years: this is believed to reflect changing patterns in immigration and the current definition of non-English-speaking background rather than a downturn in university participation. Finally, access for people with disabilities has improved, if not to the point of equality with population share, though it has to be noted that the national dataset based on institutional self-reports is less well-developed for this group (Table 3.1).

Equity issues are still to be resolved for the remaining three equity groups: people from lower socio-economic backgrounds, rural and isolated people, and indigenous people (DETYA 1999).

Table 3.1 Higher education participation by equity groups in Australia: per cent of enrolled home students, 1991 and 2001 (adapted from DEST 2002b).

Equity group	1991	2001	Reference values
People with a disability	2.0	3.1	4.0
Indigenous students	0.9	1.2	1.6/2.0 Note 1
People of non-English-speaking background	4.1	3.6	4.9/4.8 Note 1
People from rural and isolated backgrounds	20.4	19.1	28.8 Note 2
People from lower SES backgrounds	14.7	14.6	25.0 Note 3

Note 1 Reference values based on 1991 and 1996 Census data respectively
Note 2 Reference value based on data obtained from the 1991 Census
Note 3 Reference value is set at 25 per cent of the population

People from lower socio-economic backgrounds are defined as 25 per cent of the national population, yet occupy only 14.5 per cent of university places. Per capita estimates suggest that only five people from lower socio-economic backgrounds attend university for every ten people of medium or higher socio-economic backgrounds. This degree of inequity has remained relatively stable for over a decade. The situation for people from rural and isolated areas is slightly better: people living in rural or isolated Australia make up 28.8 per cent of the nation's population, yet their participation share in universities is only 19.1 per cent. For every ten urban people who attend university, six rural/isolated Australians on a per capita basis can be expected to do so. The isolated group is one of the most under-represented groups in Australian higher education and experiences poor retention rates.

Research by the Centre for the Study of Higher Education (CSHE) into the aspirations and expectations of senior secondary students has revealed some of the attitudinal differences that underpin these differential parti-cipation rates (James et al. 1999; James 2002). Students from lower socio-economic backgrounds are significantly less likely than other students to believe that a university course would offer them the chance of an inter-esting and rewarding career. Lower socio-economic background students have:

- A stronger belief that a vocational education and training (TAFE) course would be more useful to them than a university course (30 per cent believed that it would be, compared with only 14 per cent of higher socio-economic background students);
- A weaker personal interest in the subjects they could study at university (62 per cent, compared with 78 per cent);
- Less confidence that their parents want them to do a university course (44 per cent, compared with 68 per cent); and
- A stronger interest in earning an income as soon as they leave school (35 per cent, compared with 20 per cent).

In addition, students from lower socio-economic backgrounds perceive educational achievement barriers which may impede their access to higher education. These students are:

- Less confident that their academic results will be good enough for entry to courses that might interest them (38 per cent, compared with 25 per cent); and
- More likely to believe they will not have the subjects required for courses that might interest them (24 per cent, compared with 15 per cent).

The overall cost of higher education is a major deterrent for students of lower socio-economic background. Forty-one per cent of lower socio-economic background students believed their families probably could not afford the costs of supporting them at university. Well over one-third of lower socio-economic background students indicated they would have to support themselves financially if they went to university.

Overall, 'non-traditional students' are more likely to gain access to the newer universities and are less successful in the competitive entry for the more prestigious professional fields (Postle et al. 1995). People of lower socio-economic background range dramatically in population share across universities – from 5 to 45 per cent in 1999 – with a share of below 10 per cent in five of the eight older, research-intensive institutions (DETYA 2000). The research-intensive universities on average fall well below the national mean for participation share of people from lower socio-economic backgrounds, with 9.6 per cent of their students coming from lower socio-economic backgrounds compared with the national average of 14.7 per cent (and a population reference value of 25 per cent).

Indigenous people are seriously under-represented, though there has been a steady improvement in their participation share. The participation share analysis is complicated by a shifting reference point caused by a trend for more Australians to identify as indigenous (Dobson 2001). Retention and success rates for indigenous Australians are well below average, with recent estimates suggesting a completion rate of barely 50 per cent. The poor completion rate appears to be explained in part by demographic patterns in indigenous people's enrolment, including the tendency for indigenous students to be male, to be mature-age and to be enrolled externally. The universities with the highest participation rates also have the lowest success and retention rates (DETYA 1999). There is some speculation that indigenous people may withdraw from university prior to completion because they have achieved their educational goals. For some indigenous people, a period of higher education may have equipped them with community-relevant skills and there are strong pressures on them to return to their communities.

Retention: causes and trends

The vigorous pursuit of increased access and participation rates over the last decade has generated intense interest and activity aimed at improving retention rates of undergraduate students. Gaining access to university quite obviously does not guarantee the successful completion of a degree programme. Once students are selected, universities have an obligation to give them a reasonable chance of completion. The responsibility to ensure that students are able to meet course demands increasingly weighs heavily on the support structures in universities and departments, and tests the resources of individual academics. Many of the obstacles that students from disadvantaged backgrounds encounter prior to university continue to challenge their capacity to succeed from the time they are enrolled. Indeed, in some extreme instances, students depart before they actually commence classes.

While the success and retention rates for indigenous people have been consistently and unacceptably low, and while rural and isolated students enrolled externally (that is, distance education students) continue to withdraw from courses despite their success in individual subjects, the success and retention rates for other equity groups are on a par with students overall (Nelson 2003). However, focusing only on the retention rates of defined access groups overlooks the complexity of the patterns and causes of non-completion in Australian universities. Generally speaking, the social mix of Australian universities has for some time been more representative of the general population than in most countries (Anderson and Vervoorn 1983). The diversity of student motives and shifting policy perspectives has presented definitional issues for retention studies. The term 'dropout' is still used occasionally, but more neutral terms such as 'attrition', 'discontinuance', 'withdrawal' and 'non-completion' currently appear as interchangeable. Completion rates are a constant source of debate, much of it on shaky grounds since it is hard to pin down with any precision the number of students who actually disappear from higher education altogether. The pattern of shifting enrolments across universities, or changing courses within institutions, is difficult to monitor.

A review of research and development on non-completion in Australia (McInnis, Hartley et al. 2000) forms the basis of the discussion that follows. In that review, the working definition of non-completion refers to students who commence study but do not gain a university qualification. At an institutional level, this definition is not particularly meaningful since it begs the question as to when a student can legitimately be said to have departed entirely. One university, for example, classifies students who do not re-enrol after first year as: 'transferred' (to another course at the same or another university); 'lapsed' (students who disappear without notice); and, 'discontinued' (those who withdraw voluntarily or at the request of a faculty). From the perspective of government and institutions there is nevertheless concern about inefficiencies and wastage even for those students who leave part-way through a course but eventually complete some qualification well beyond the normal progress rate.

The difficulties in understanding the patterns of, and reasons for, discontinuation are magnified by the limited data sources in Australia. There are few longitudinal studies with sufficient focus to inform policy and practice, and little is known about the trigger points for and process of withdrawal. Nor is there much information about withdrawal in later years. In contrast much attention has been given to the first year experience and to the concerns of specific equity groups. Most Australian work on retention draws on studies of students in their first year of undergraduate study since this is the point at which many students are vulnerable. Interest in later year departures is now emerging (Krause et al. 2002) as interest in the effectiveness of professionally oriented degree programmes with practical work experience raises questions about their impact on student performance and persistence.

An analysis of longitudinal data of undergraduate completion rates by the Commonwealth Department of Education, Science and Training (Martin et al. 2001) shows that, of the students who commenced in 1992, 64 per cent had completed an award at the same university by 1999. However, in Australian universities, many students change degree programmes mid-stream. Since the fairly flexible course structures in many fields encourage students to keep their options open on commencement, it is not surprising that students are able to take up new programmes with some credits. Likewise, a significant and increasing number of students enrol in combined bachelor degree programmes such as Arts/Law or Arts/Engineering, and, for a variety of reasons, some simply discontinue one of the two degrees. Clearly, the proportion of students who complete the degree they started is lower than the overall completion rate. When rates are calculated to include students who completed a degree at another university, the final national completion rate is around 70 per cent. Some of the demographic differences in completion rates are striking. The Commonwealth study found that higher completion rates are associated with: women; full-time students; younger students; and students who entered with a year 12 tertiary entrance score.[19]

Importantly, the analysis noted a great deal of variation in completion rates across fields of study.

Institutional interest in retention issues has been heightened by government use of student progress rates as a performance indicator but since completion rates present problems at the institutional level, a measure called the Student Progress Unit (SPU) has been developed to measure student success in completing subjects in relation to the subjects in which they enrolled. Dobson and Sharma (1993) argue that, in the Australian context at least, this is a better measure of student progress than course completion. The problem of tracking students from one university to another across the system remains. As it stands, the accuracy of institutional data varies across institutions.

Major findings from Australian research

The findings of retention studies in Australia generally mirror those of the UK (for example, Yorke et al. 1997), although it should be understood that a number of aspects distinguish the Australian experience from that of the UK or, indeed, the US with respect to non-completion. There is, for example, a low level of student mobility across the country, students tend to go to a university near their home city and most stay at home for at least the initial years of their study. The minority of students in residential halls have a quite different set of support structures and a distinctive experience. There is also a much stronger vocational focus in Australian universities and, in contrast to the US, there is no great interest in the civic or spiritual growth of students, with the exception of some residential colleges.

Moreover, the system is distinctive for its established tradition of diversity in the student population, with large proportions of mature-age entry, external and distance education, and part-time students. Australian students have for many years been able to move in and out of higher education depending on their life-stage needs and aspirations.

Much of the current Australian policy discussion about the relationship between the quality of the student experience and non-completion relies on the evidence from first year students who in fact remain on course but with a strong sense of uncertainty (McInnis and James 1995; McInnis, Hartley et al. 2000). The results of these surveys tend to be used as pointers to the factors that influence students to withdraw, simply because it is so difficult and costly to track students who discontinue. It might be argued that the real test of motives is actual departure rather than thinking about it but, on the whole, the factors that cause students to seriously consider withdrawing in the first year are much the same as those found in the large-scale surveys of students who had actually left.

Almost 35 per cent of first year students in the two surveys had seriously considered deferring in the first six months of their study (McInnis and James 1995; McInnis, James et al. 2000). Their reasons for uncertainty about their enrolment revealed again the diversity and complexity of their contexts. University-related reasons were mentioned more frequently than non-university-related reasons. Overall, disliking study, disliking the course, or wanting to change course appeared more common than health, family, employment and similar reasons. The reasons clustered together. For example, students who mentioned emotional health were more likely to include financial problems, disliking their course and disliking study. One result of the survey that has had a major impact on institutional responses considered below, is that a much higher proportion of students who had considered deferring had not made close friends at university, kept to themselves, and were not interested in extra-curricular activities.

Making choices

The expansion of the higher education system and the range of choice available in a market competition environment has generated a great deal of pressure on students to make informed choices about which course and which university. Career choice in Australia is perhaps a more critical factor for young undergraduates since the national pattern is for undergraduates to be vocationally focused from the first year. Without a liberal or general education as a prerequisite, most students start university with a career path in mind. First year students who are both uncertain about their choice of course or university, and dissatisfied with their initial experience, are far less likely than most to have come to university with a career in mind. They are also less clear about why they had come to university at all (McInnis and James 1995).

The fact is that many students do not take the trouble to inform themselves about the options available. Making 'wrong' choices as a factor in discontinuation is not, however, as clear as it might seem – certainly not in an open and flexible system in Australia where students can usually take credits with them and advanced standing in degrees is often available. In some cases 'wrong choices' are the product of bad advice – or none – but may equally arise because students and their parents choose to ignore good advice. For some of these people, withdrawal from a course can be traumatic and regarded as an opportunity cost, but for others, it was never time wasted since they may have gathered what they needed to start in a new direction. Likewise, in universities where selective admission is the norm, many students take a second preference course to give themselves a second chance of entry to their preferred field of study. It is not uncommon in the process for these students to turn their second preference into a new and successful pathway.

Adjusting to university

Some students find the first year a daunting, intimidating and alienating experience. Lack of readiness to cope with the demands of university study is often the source of these experiences and amplifies the doubts that students may have. The national surveys of first year students (McInnis and James 1995; McInnis, James et al. 2000) found that almost 29 per cent of students said they had difficulty adjusting to the style of teaching at university. Around 45 per cent of students say they found the standard of work required at university much higher than they expected, and 57 per cent thought university study was more demanding than school. These and related results highlight the vulnerability of first year students in the transition process. The impact of the quality of teaching on decisions to leave is not clear. There is little reference in the Australian research to suggest that poor teaching plays a significant role in student decisions to leave. Likewise there is little evidence that overcrowded classrooms and the associated resource deficiencies are important. It is worth noting, however, that a substantial proportion of first year students say they are getting marks lower than they expected, and that these students are more likely to be negative about the quality of teaching. Which of the two factors is the primary contributor to early departure is difficult to say: common sense says that both readily combine with other factors to compound a negative experience. In contrast, it is also true that students who are highly committed to their course and career are likely to tolerate poor teaching and working conditions.

The impact of personal reasons

The research shows consistently that it is unusual for students to cite just one factor influencing their decision to leave. Distinguishing conceptually between so-called 'personal' and institutional reasons for non-completion does not make a lot of sense in reality. Case studies give better insights on these dynamics than large-scale surveys. Schedvin (1985), for example, found five groups of sometimes overlapping reasons for students discontinuing in a health sciences course: commitment to a prior goal; the need for 'time out'; the desire to reality-test a career; specific academic difficulties that generated a strong fear of failure; and a range of factors beyond the control of the student such as illness, family crisis or financial pressure. Students in the first category are responding to selective admissions processes. Students who are not successful in gaining their first preference in highly sought courses are at risk of continuing in a consolation-prize course with a considerable amount of dissatisfaction and absence of the commitment that might otherwise have pulled them through times of personal crisis. For these students, the typical 'moments of doubt' that many students experience as a matter of routine are sufficient to prompt abrupt and early discontinuation. Schedvin observed that students' accounts of their situations illustrated the often complex interplay of personal, social and family reasons for having chosen a particular course in the first place that then impact on a student's decision to withdraw. The notion of reality-testing is a particularly salient factor in professional courses such as health sciences where aptitudes such as interpersonal skills play a significant role.

Health and relationship problems are a consistent theme in the research, but it is unusual for these alone to be the cause of withdrawal from a course except where there is a major trauma such as a bereavement or critical illness. However, for students with low levels of motivation and commitment, even minor illnesses or personal crises can be linked with other trigger factors to bring uncertainty to a head. As noted above, students who mention health as an influence on their thinking are also more likely to refer to financial problems, disliking their course and disliking study entirely. There is of course considerable diversity in terms of life-stages as to which factors are likely to combine to provoke the decision to leave.

Financial factors and the impact of part-time work

A national study of student income (Long and Hayden 2001) found strong evidence that students' financial circumstances are having an impact on their studies. The HECS system described above means that most undergraduate students are not burdened by fees while doing their degree. In contrast to the United States, only 11 per cent of the students surveyed said they had obtained a loan in order to be able to continue their studies. The average loan was around $AUS4000 and most students in this category were from disadvantaged backgrounds. While Long and Hayden did not directly explore the relationship between financial difficulties and retention, their findings support the conclusions of the first year studies (McInnis and James 1995; McInnis, James et al. 2000) that full-time students are working longer part-time hours and spending less time on campus.

The impact of paid part-time work on student retention has been the subject of considerable discussion in the last few years but the evidence is far from clear-cut. A national study of full-time students managing study and paid work (McInnis and Hartley 2002) did not find a clear association between hours of part-time work and grades, but did identify a number of aspects of part-time work that put students at risk. Paid work is now the only or main source of income for most students, although not all work to meet the necessities of life. It is worth noting that the financial allowance schemes in place are actually structured in such a way as to be a disincentive for students to work more than one day a week.

The average engagement in part-time work by full-time students in Australia is around 15 hours per week. This is three times the hours worked by students in 1984 and the trend is on the increase. However, the hours of work are less significant than is generally thought. So long as students are capable time-managers, are motivated to learn, and are involved in university life they are not especially at risk of failing or leaving. Conversely, some important and overlooked indirect negative effects of part-time work include the absence of friends and social networks, a lack of a sense of student identity, and no involvement in extra-curricular activities: the direct consequences of this scenario for retention are yet to be explored. It is likely that the diminished quality of the student experience makes the decision to leave somewhat easier. Students who take on too much work, skip classes, worry about money and feel overwhelmed by all they have to do are most at risk of repeated failure and discontinuing.

Part-time enrolment and discontinuation

Managing the quality of the part-time or external student experience has been a quite separate and long-standing challenge for Australian universities. While the system actively encourages people in full-time employment or with family responsibilities to enrol, it is still the case that these students are amongst the most likely to withdraw from their studies. As a group, their attrition rate is estimated to be double that for full-time undergraduates. The biggest difference in academic performance between on-campus and off-campus students occurs in the first year, where they are most vulnerable (Long 1994). The reasons for their discontinuation are not all that different from on-campus full-time students, although the results are mixed. Brown (1995) established that insufficient support from tutors and difficulty in contacting them were major contributing factors. Only students who left because they had changed jobs did so wholly for what could be termed factors external to the university. At least part of the problem rests with students who are too ambitious or impatient and take on more subjects than they should. Many of them expect to return at some stage.

Institutional factors: local conditions

In reality, the causes of non-completion described above are played in different ways across different institutions. A plethora of institutional studies in recent years have looked to local factors in the hope of providing some guidance for strategic intervention. Ramsay et al. (1996) surveyed all commencing undergraduate students who withdrew from the University of South Australia, comparing them with a control group of students who persisted. The university is well-known for its flexible admissions policies and its support for equity groups, and mature-age students. The major reasons for withdrawal were identified as a mix of personal, employment and financial issues, academic preparation and the course itself. While this is not surprising, it is the variations in the importance of the reasons across the equity groups that was informative at the institutional level. It was found, for example, that external and indigenous students who withdrew were least likely to make use of general support services.

A recent study at La Trobe University in Victoria (Blunden 2002) illustrates the importance of local conditions. The overall attrition rate in a representative sample of subjects surveyed was about 20 per cent. The study included only students who had been enrolled with a year 12 score and thus excluded mature-age or special entry students. Interestingly, the study showed only a 'trend' towards a correlation between higher entry scores, student results and persistence, but this was by no means universally the case. Amongst the themes observed from responses to a survey of students, three were especially noteworthy: students found the subject matter 'too difficult, excessive, or irrelevant'; they suffered from 'lack or preparedness'; and, reflecting the particular student population, they found their work being adversely affected by part-time paid work commitments.

A study of the 'new' outer urban campus of the University of Western Sydney (Grierson and Parr 1994) provides an example of specific local difficulties contributing to high early departure rates. The relatively low status at that time of the university in terms of student preferences was exacerbated by the outer urban geographic isolation of the campus. Student withdrawal was highest at the beginning of the year with three subgroups of departing students: those who transferred to another institution after successfully completing a year at UWS; those who withdrew early in the first semester because of dissatisfaction with courses; and, those who withdrew because of course failure. Two of the most common reasons for withdrawal relevant to the UWS context were: leaving to attend another institution; and problems of distance or travel.

Institutional strategies for reducing non-completion

It is important to recognize from the analysis of reasons for discontinuation that there are limits to intervention and the need to focus on what institutions can do to make a difference. There is very little systematic evaluation of the effectiveness of the approaches outlined below. Much of the work is focused on inputs and levels of usage. A study by Sharma and Burgess (1994) came to the noteworthy conclusion that institutions should not expend too many resources in trying to overcome attrition problems since, from their analysis, only 18 per cent of the students they surveyed believed that the institution could have influenced their decision. Nevertheless, accountability pressures on universities and the application of retention as a performance indicator has changed the policy dynamic, and institutions are now responding in substantial and creative ways to develop schemes to keep attrition to a minimum.

The institutional strategies to minimize withdrawal in the early years of undergraduate and non-completion generally can be grouped into five kinds of responses: a focus on student marketing and recruitment; transition management; rethinking approaches to teaching and learning; developing more sophisticated student support programmes and infrastructure; and the development of learning communities.

Australian universities have responded to the issues raised about retention in the first year with major efforts to improve the quality and accuracy of information provided to prospective students. Most have taken steps to rethink their marketing and recruitment processes to minimize confusion and the likelihood of a negative cycle of dissatisfaction and departure. Much of this effort is now linked to quite sophisticated transition programmes with substantial investment by most universities in student orientation programmes.

A key part of the transition management process is the communication of university expectations of students. Lack of clarity in goals and objectives simply exacerbates the negative views of the uncertain starters. The suite of activities to ensure students adjust effectively to university study grows every year. Preparatory, bridging and foundation courses operate in a variety of forms, mostly directed at closing the gap between the knowledge and academic skills that students bring with them and the requirements of the university. There is, however, growing resistance to remedial programmes that attempt to make up for the work that should have been done by schools. A number of fields of study are now developing '101' subjects in the US tradition. A voluntary, or in some cases, compulsory 101 subject in an

Australian university might require students to attend a flexibly timetabled one hour session each week. It has a study-group orientation and focuses on helping students adjust to learning at university generally as well as issues specific to the field of study. A common element in most 101 programmes is the provision of a cohort experience. In faculties with large enrolments this has a considerable and positive impact on student sense of belonging and identity. Students are encouraged to share resources, form networks with other students, and develop the confidence to seek help and advice from academic staff. Students who participate appear to adapt more easily to university life, and are more likely to persist beyond the first months of their course. The evidence so far is that they have been successful in addressing the major problem of diversity of educational backgrounds in the classroom.

A major thrust throughout all universities has been a rethinking of approaches to teaching and learning in the early years. Universities and academics now recognize that the 'sink or swim' practices of the past are inappropriate. The general themes of reforms and innovations include: conscious efforts to assist a shift in students' learning approaches towards more independent and self-directed learning; new approaches to assessment practices; and, particularly, a strong agenda to improve the timing and quality of feedback students get on their academic progress. Alongside these efforts there are now more sophisticated student support programmes and infrastructure that, amongst other things, identify students at risk of failing or departing.

Finally, there has been a broad acceptance of the importance of students becoming connected or engaged with the university as a key strategy in improving retention. On average, around a quarter of students do not make friends of any significance in their first year at university (McInnis and James 1995) and this pattern then continues into subsequent years. As a direct result, student mentoring and peer support programmes are widespread and, although they range in sophistication and effectiveness, it is now assumed that students will be given every opportunity to develop a sense of collective identity and belonging. Overcoming the potentially debilitating effects of social isolation in the many large campuses of Australian universities is an ongoing cause for concern.

4

Access and retention in English higher education: a parliamentary perspective

Tensions

Finifter et al. (1991) introduced the idea of 'the uneasy triangle' into macroeconomics in order to illustrate the tension between three competing goals – economic growth, full employment and price stability. All three could not be maximally achieved at the same time, and hence trade-offs had to be made. There is something of a similarity with higher education, where the desire is for the system simultaneously to deliver – in fairly crude terms – high quality, widen access and engender high levels of completion.[20] This is a considerable challenge.

The House of Commons Select Committee on Education and Employment[21] investigated access and retention in 2000–2001, and exposed clearly the tension between widening participation and retention. Its successor Select Committee returned in 2002 to the thorny matter of post-16 student support. This chapter summarizes, and comments on, some of the main points at issue. It also touches on two investigations carried out by the National Audit Office into much the same topics. Before considering these investigations, it is necessary to sketch some of the background for readers who are unfamiliar with the development of higher education in the UK in recent years.

Expansion of the sector

The UK higher education sector expanded greatly[22] during the latter part of the Thatcher/Major Conservative administration, the growth having been given impetus by the then Secretary of State for Education, Kenneth Baker[23] (see Longden 2000 for a more detailed discussion relating to this period of expansion). The number of full-time undergraduates in the system rose from 553,000 to 1,162,000 between 1982–83 and 1997–98, with part-time enrolments up from 297,000 to 541,000 over the same period.[24]

However, the expansion put pressure on public finances since the higher education institutions had to be funded to create the extra places, and the increased number of full-time students were eligible (subject to an audit of their means) for maintenance awards from the state.[25] Some of the expansion was on a 'fees only' basis (that is, institutions received no additional 'core' funding for their infrastructural needs), and the unit of funding – the funding per full-time equivalent student – steadily declined through most of the 1990s, flattening out at just over £5000 from 1997–98 (Figure 4.1). Although the unit of funding has been roughly constant from 1997–98, this hides an increase in national expenditure deriving from the increased numbers of students in the system: the increase from 1997–98 to 2003–2004 is approximately £1 billion at 2001–2002 prices, or around 20 per cent.

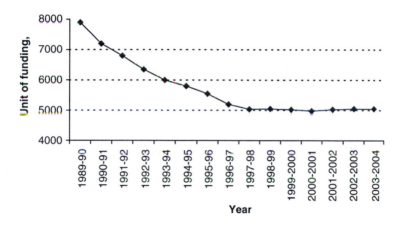

Figure 4.1 Unit of funding (£ per full-time equivalent student) from 1989–90 to 2003–2004 (DfES 2003a: para. 1.31)

The unhappiness in the sector regarding the declining unit of resource indicated institutions' worries about their capacity to fulfil the expectations laid upon them, including the provision of the quality of the student experience for which higher education in the UK had a high reputation (see Longden 2001a for an extended discussion on the contested terrain of funding higher education). Questions were asked of the sector regarding the maintenance of quality and standards and, although the assessments of teaching quality that were undertaken by the national Funding Councils[26] gave a generally clean bill of health to academic provision, concern over the declining unit of resource was never wholly able to allay them. During its investigations, the Select Committee heard evidence to the effect that a combination of the declining unit of resource, larger teaching groups and the pressure on academics to perform well in research was adversely affecting the quality of the student experience. However, in his evidence to the Committee, Sir Howard Newby (then Chief Executive Designate of

HEFCE) urged that to infer a correlation between the quality of teaching and the eminence of academic staff would be simplistic.[27]

The issues of retention and completion had begun to emerge as matters of policy importance during this decade as discussions took place regarding the performance indicators that would be appropriate for the sector that had been unified in 1992. These will also have gained salience because of the public cost implications. The rate of non-completion rose from 13 per cent in 1982–83 to 17 per cent in 1997–98, but – as noted earlier – over the same period the number of full-time undergraduates had more than doubled. It was perhaps no coincidence that in 1996 HEFCE commissioned a group in the north-west of England to conduct a study of retention and its costs (reported as Yorke et al. 1997).

In 1996 the increasingly difficult issue of resourcing higher education prompted the then Conservative administration in the UK and its main opposition party (Labour) to agree to establish a National Committee of Inquiry into Higher Education under the chairmanship of Sir Ron (later, Lord) Dearing. This had the political advantage to both sides of their not having to deal with what was bound to be a tricky issue of public policy in the run up to the 1997 general election.

When the National Committee reported in July 1997 (by which time the new Labour government had taken office), it put forward four options to replace the existing system,[28] as is shown in Table 4.1. The Committee was sensitive to the position of students from low-income backgrounds, and discussed the implications of its options for them (NCIHE 1997: paras 20.55ff).

Table 4.1 Options put forward by the National Committee (NCIHE 1997: para. 20.45).

	Living costs support	Tuition contribution
Existing system	50% means-tested grant; 50% loan	None
Option A Maintenance contribution	100% income-contingent loan	None
Option B Tuition contribution	50% means-tested grant; 50% income-contingent loan	25% contribution with income-contingent loan
Option C Means-tested tuition contribution	100% income-contingent loan	25% means-tested contribution with no loan
Option D Tuition contribution with restoration of maintenance grants	100% means-tested grant	25% contribution with income-contingent loan

The incoming Labour government, however, decided against implementing the National Committee's recommendation for an income-contingent repayment of a contribution (of around 25 per cent) to the average cost of tuition, and instead to replace student grants with loans and introduce a flat-rate, 'up front' contribution to tuition fees.

The Education and Employment Select Committee's inquiries, 2000–2001

Within two years of the funding changes introduced in 1997 by the incoming government, the then Chair of the Education and Employment Select Committee, Malcolm Wicks, established an inquiry into higher education. The Chair of a Select Committee has the right to determine its agenda, and Wicks' choice suggests that there was a growing concern amongst parliamentary backbenchers about the impact being made by the chosen funding policy. The successor Select Committee, that on Education and Skills, made this very explicit in its report on *Post-16 Student Support* (House of Commons 2002).

In July 1999 the brief for the inquiry was issued (House of Commons 1999), with its main focus being on the student experience. Wicks' successor as Chair, Barry Sheerman, took the opportunity to extend the remit of the inquiry to deal with widened participation in higher education and student retention, the latter of which had emerged as a policy concern (House of Commons 2000). It was clear that the Select Committee anticipated that the financing of higher education institutions and the support system for students would gain further public attention, and it saw its deliberations as 'helping to set the agenda for debate' (House of Commons 2001b: para. 8).

At an early stage in setting the agenda the Select Committee decided to conduct the inquiry – which, because devolution had by now begun to affect the UK, did not encompass Scotland and Northern Ireland – under two separate headings: the first part of the inquiry focused on access into higher education and gave rise to the Fourth Report (House of Commons 2001b), whereas the second focused on retention and gave rise to the Sixth Report (House of Commons 2001c). The government replied to the recommendations regarding student access and retention (House of Commons 2001a, 2001d).

Access

In a Memorandum to the Select Committee, HEFCE indicated that participation in higher education had widened considerably over the preceding two decades, but that there was still under-representation of young people from poor backgrounds and from some specific ethnic minority groups (House of Commons 2001b: 86 [paras 3–4]). Whereas in the late 1990s around 50 per cent of the UK population was categorized as socio-economic groups (SEGs) IIIm to V (skilled manual, semi-skilled and unskilled), only 25 per cent of entrants to higher education came from these groups (HEFCE 1999a: 8). The Council had taken a number of initiatives to improve the position (summarized in House of Commons 2001b: 88ff [Annex A]).

The Select Committee was aware of the 'very close correlation between social background and educational achievement prior to university entrance' (House of Commons 2001b: xiii [para. 28]), and expressed its desire that initiatives to improve success prior to higher education should themselves succeed – amongst these were the 'outreach' activities conducted by some higher education institutions whose aim was to attract pupils who might otherwise not consider education after they had left school. The Committee was also concerned that pre-entry 'summer schools' should reach out to under-represented groups and not merely act as enrichment activities for the already privileged.

Retention and completion

In 2000 the UK government indicated that its commitment to expanding and widening participation in higher education should not be accompanied by lower levels of programme completion. The annual letter by the Secretary of State for Education and Employment to the Chairman of HEFCE stated, in paragraph 11:

> Notwithstanding progress on recruitment, institutions should focus on retaining students, particularly those from disadvantaged backgrounds. Widening access to higher education must not lead to an increase in the number of people who fail to complete their courses. I therefore expect to see the Council bear down on the rate of 'drop out'. The evidence shows there are unacceptable variations in the rate of 'drop out' which appear to be linked more to the culture and workings of the institution than to the background or nature of the students recruited. It is therefore time for much more substantial work to be done on identifying best practice and bringing pressure to bear on those institutions whose performance falls significantly below their benchmark.
>
> (Blunkett 2000)

The Select Committee went along with the general tenor of this view, saying that institutions should not accept as students those 'with no chance of obtaining any credit for their higher education study' (House of Commons 2001c: x [para. 14]). The distinction between 'any credit' and programme completion should be noted, since the Committee was concerned that intermediate achievements should be more portable within the sector (House of Commons 2001c: ix–x, xii [paras 13, 14, 25]).

Data provided by HEFCE to the Education and Employment Select Committee showed that the incidence of non-continuation following the year of entry was related to socio-economic group (Table 4.2). A subsequent tabulation in the same Memorandum (House of Commons 2001c: 122), using 'benchmarks' catering for entry qualification and subject profile, showed that the influence of social class on non-continuation was relatively small. However, with class and qualification being correlated, it is unclear how much of the variation in non-continuation that can be attributed to class has been 'partialled out' in the computation of the benchmarks. Put another way, the effect of class may have been partially submerged.

Table 4.2 Percentage non-continuation following year of entry by social class and entry qualifications, for young full-time first degree entrants in 1997–98. (Source: House of Commons 2001c: 121)

Social class	High A-Level entry	Mid A-Level entry	Low A-Level entry	Not A-Level entry	All entrants
I	2	5	10	10	5
II	3	6	11	11	6
IIIn	3	6	11	13	7
IIIm	3	6	11	13	8
IV and V	3	7	12	13	9

The picture is reflected in the institution-level performance data from HEFCE (2002). Figure 4.2 illustrates the relationship between the proportion of students from lower socio-economic groups and non-continuation following the first year full-time first degree study. The correlation (Pearson r) between these two variables is 0.79. While this cannot be claimed to be a causal relationship, such a strong relationship invites further investigation.

What the data in Table 4.2 do not show is that there is a strong relationship in England between deprivation (as indexed by the proportion of pupils entitled to free school meals) and average A-Level points score ($r = -0.54$). The relationship is at its strongest in regions with large conurbations, such as the north-east (-0.76) and north-west (-0.67) of England, Yorkshire and Humberside (-0.74), and London (-0.62), and at its weakest in the south-west (-0.06).[29] Thus pupils from deprived areas[30] are more likely to obtain weak A-Level grades and hence are at greater risk of non-completion. This dismal picture is actually worse, in that pupils from deprived backgrounds are less likely than their more advantaged peers to continue schooling to A-Level in the first place.

At the other end of the spectrum of privilege, Naylor and Smith (2002) showed that pupils from fee-paying schools, when compared with those with equivalent qualifications from state schools, obtained on average a *lower*

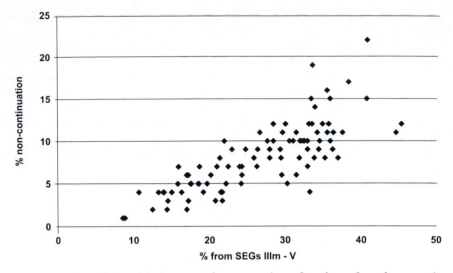

Figure 4.2   The relationship between the proportion of students from lower socio-economic groups and percentage non-continuation in the year following entry

class of degree when graduating from UK universities in 1993.[31] This – perhaps counter-intuitive – finding may partly be attributable to independent school pupils being better prepared by their teachers for the A-Level examinations, but not necessarily better prepared for learning in higher education.

Influences on retention and completion

At the time of the Select Committee's investigations there was little to indicate why some institutions were outperforming their benchmarks for completion and others were underperforming in this respect. Sir Howard Newby, commenting on the institutional performance data computed by HEFCE, said:

> There were not any obvious correlations between ... factors ... such as size or whether they are old or new universities or anything of that kind. It appears to rest very much on factors which are particular to a particular institution rather than across a range of institutions.
>
> (House of Commons 2001c: 61 [para. 185])

The studies sponsored by the Funding Council's Action on Access Team subsequently addressed the issue of how some institutions were being conspicuously successful as regards student success, or were working to that end (see Chapter 9).

The Select Committee received conflicting messages about the influence of financial considerations on completion.[32] Bahram Bekhradnia (then

Director of Policy at HEFCE) suggested that financial issues might be secondary to academic considerations. Other witnesses indicated that students' need to take part-time employment was affecting their academic performance, and that financial pressures were felt most acutely by students from the lower socio-economic groups (both in terms of raw debt and in terms of the higher number of hours they spent on part-time employment). Evidence was provided that disabled students were at a disadvantage because of delays in securing the Disabled Students Allowance and of difficulties in obtaining part-time employment. The Committee took the view that it would be self-defeating to seek to prevent part-time employment by students from relatively poor backgrounds unless financial support for them were to be increased.

The investigations undertaken by the National Audit Office

At about the same time as the Education and Employment Select Committee was conducting its work, the National Audit Office, which reports to the House of Commons on matters relating to the economy, efficiency and effectiveness with which departments and other bodies have used publicly funded resources, undertook an audit of university value for money which focused on access-related issues and student achievement. Two reports, paralleling the Select Committee's reports, were published in January 2002, that relating to student achievement appearing as National Audit Office (2002a), and that on access as National Audit Office (2002b). The second discusses representation in higher education, pointing out – *inter alia* – that students from lower socio-economic groups and those with disabilities were still considerably under-represented in higher education, and discussed ways in which this might be ameliorated.

The report on achievement (which covered retention and employment) is the more germane to the theme of this book. It drew substantially from existing sources of statistics, complementing these by a survey of institutions. The NAO also commissioned interviews with 26 former students and with eight focus groups involving 60 students in four institutions, exploring their experiences of higher education.

The report's reliance on the reasons students officially gave for non-completion is questionable, since students are expected to give one reason (and, as is widely appreciated, non-completion is rarely so straightforward). The two dominant reasons recorded are the 'catch-all' 'personal reasons' and academic failure. To these were added, from the interviews with ex-students, lack of preparedness, changes in personal circumstances, financial difficulties, the impact of part-time working, and dissatisfaction with the course or the institution. No student said that the quality of teaching was a main factor in the decision, but a number of teaching-related issues were mentioned, such as feedback on work. It is unclear from the report how the respondents construed 'teaching': it is a matter for conjecture as to whether they understood teaching in a limited sense, such as lecturing and leading tutorials.

Whilst the two reports made interesting reading, their heavy reliance on existing sources meant that they were able to add relatively little to contemporary understanding of both access and student achievement.

The Education and Skills Select Committee investigation, 2002

As noted earlier, the issue of student support has been a hot political topic for some time, not least because of its electoral implications. Prompted by remarks made by the Prime Minister at the Labour Party Conference of 2001, which indicated that a wide-ranging review of student finance was in the offing (Blair 2001), the Education and Skills Select Committee (which had replaced the Education and Employment Select Committee) decided that an investigation on its part would make a useful contribution.

The Committee concluded that the government's rapid rejection of the recommendations of the Dearing Report (NCIHE 1997) and the introduction of its own preferred approach to student support had been inappropriate and had led to difficulties. The current system of student support had failed in three respects (House of Commons 2001c: para. 74):

- It had had no significant impact on the level of participation by those from lower socio-economic groups;
- It was poorly understood by the target populations; and
- It was not socially equitable and 'progressive' (meaning that the system did not give the less well-off a disproportionately greater 'helping hand' to overcome their disadvantage).

The Committee was concerned that the system of income-contingent loans was insufficiently discriminating in favour of those who had the greatest need. An interest rate of effectively zero enabled those with financial resources to profit by investing their loans. The Committee recommended to the government a series of financial measures that it thought would reduce the disadvantage experienced by those from lower socio-economic groups, including a system of student support based on interest rates that could be varied according to national priorities and economic conditions, and loans that reflected the real costs of pursuing a course of study.

The funding of institutions was a matter of continuing concern, and the funding of infrastructure should not be prejudiced by the funding given to student support. The Committee did not take a position on the differentiation of fees by subject and/or institution, which remains an issue of debate between parties with rather different interests.

Funding retention?

Retention and completion could be improved in institutions if greater attention were given to overcoming the disadvantages with which some students embark on higher education. As the Education and Skills Select Committee argued, much could be done by revisions to the system of student support.

A second line of approach would be to improve the quality of their experience as students. To do this, though, implies the need for additional institutional resources – especially of relatively expensive staff time. The need had been recognized by the introduction in England of a 5 per cent funding premium (subsequently raised to 10 per cent) for students who originated from areas whose postcodes correlated with indices of deprivation.[33] The latter figure was found to be inadequate for the purpose and, following recommendations from the Education and Employment Select Committee (House of Commons 2001b: xx [para. 64]) and its successor the Education and Skills Select Committee (House of Commons 2001c: 13 [para. 33]), the government has proposed that it be raised to 20 per cent for English higher education in 2003–2004 (DfES 2003a: para. 6.25).[34] However, the Committee was disappointed to find that the increased premium would be funded by a reallocation of existing resources rather than by 'new money' (House of Commons 2003: para. 135).

As discussion of the financing of the National Health Service has shown, any assumption that additional resources will as a matter of course ameliorate problems is simplistic. *How* the resources are used is also important. For example, the way in which teachers interact with, and support, students is critically important, as the testimonies of withdrawn students presented in Chapter 8 illustrate.[35] If additional resources are diverted towards research, on the grounds that an improved rating in the next Research Assessment Exercise will bring yet more funding into the institution, the 'trickle-down' effect of this may run so slowly and thinly that there is little effect on institutional performance as far as retention and completion are concerned.

Towards the 2003 White Paper

The experience of Labour Party candidates when canvassing during the June 2001 election campaign indicated that problems relating to student support, epitomized by concerns about student debt, remained a pressing issue of public policy. As noted above, the Prime Minister had dealt with the growing pressure regarding student debt by announcing that the government would conduct a review of higher education funding. The news, while being welcomed, adumbrated a significant reversal of existing policy with regard to student support and to higher education funding in general.

Reporting on the conference, Woodward described the decision to establish a review as the first signal of a U-turn on policy (Woodward 2001). A few days later Estelle Morris,[36] the newly appointed Secretary of State for Education and Skills reaffirmed the decision to conduct a review of higher education to ensure that access to higher education was able to 'unlock the potential of the poorer sections of society' and to 'support excellent teaching in our higher education institutions' (Morris 2001). She confirmed the government's intention to maintain the participation target of 50 per cent of young people experiencing higher education by 2010, whilst recognizing that the goal would be difficult to achieve. Later in her speech she linked this goal with the need to review the system of student financial support, thereby acknowledging the concern expressed by the National Union of Students, academic staff, parents and students themselves.

Four clear aims for the review were identified as:

- Simplification of the system of student support;
- Provision of more 'up front' support for students from less well-off backgrounds;
- Ensuring student access to financial support throughout their period of study; and
- Tackling the problems of debt and perceived debt aversion.

During the period between November 2001 and May 2002 the Department for Education and Skills was engaged in an extensive data collection exercise to assist in their aim to clarify higher education policy. The results of the survey (DfES 2003b) revealed a widespread criticism of the current system of student funding, which was seen as creating potential problems regarding retention and completion. Those from lower socio-economic groups were concerned about the impact of 'up front' tuition charges discouraging students from starting on, or continuing, their studies.

The 2003 White Paper

Since the funding of institutions and of students had not been satisfactorily resolved by the changes introduced in 1997, the government planned that a White Paper on higher education in England should appear early in 2002. However, it was finally published in January 2003, and set out the government's current thinking about higher education policy. Many commentators saw the delay in publication as further evidence of a tension within government over the financial support for students and institutions (both of which had stimulated considerable debate), and the implications of any policy decisions for, *inter alia*, the widening of access and student retention.

The White Paper reaffirmed the need for reform of the English higher education system in order to retain its competitiveness. Competitiveness – and a civilized society – implied more improvement in access from lower socio-economic groups than had so far been achieved. Regarding access, the White Paper commented

> The social class gap among those entering higher education is unacceptably wide. Those from the top three social classes are almost three times as likely to enter higher education as those from the bottom three.
>
> (DfES 2003a: para. 1.28)

Although the relative rates of participation have narrowed over a period of 40 years, Figure 4.3 shows that the absolute rise in participation rate for socio-economic groups I – IIIn has been greater than that for socio-economic groups IIIm – V.[37] Data presented in House of Commons (House of Commons 2001c: 19) shows that the participation is heavily correlated with socio-economic group, with 81 per cent of young people from professional backgrounds (SEG I) participating compared with 15 per cent of those from unskilled backgrounds (SEG V).

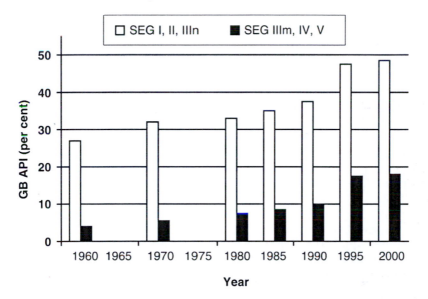

Figure 4.3 Higher education participation (age participation index) in Great Britain, 1960–2000, by broad socio-economic groups. (Source: DfES 2003a: para. 1.28)

The quality of the student experience is stressed in the White Paper, not least because the proposals for a sharp increase in fees would, if implemented, be bound to strengthen the consumer-like aspects of the student role. It is expected that students will have available to them a higher standard of information about the various aspects of programmes than they do at present, so that they can make well-informed choices. The White Paper notes that staff-student ratios (SSRs) have fallen from 1:10 in 1983 to 1:18 in

2000, and there has been a concomitant decline in face-to-face contact with staff (DfES 2003a: para. 1.19). From the point of view of the student experience, it is a pity that the SSR issue was not analysed more thoroughly, since the figures quoted appear to be gross institutional ratios which do not take into account the fact that many staff counted as academics do not occupy teaching roles in their institutions. In other words, the ratios 'on the ground' are likely to be considerably worse.

Another point made in the same paragraph connects the decline in SSR with a decrease in the writing of assignments. During this period, most of English higher education became modularized and/or semesterized. One of the consequences was that, in many institutions, the number of summative assessments was markedly increased and – of critical importance – the amount of formative assessment sharply declined. This is an issue which is exercising a number of institutions (not least because of the implications for retention), and is the subject of comment in Chapters 9 and 10.

Proposals bearing on retention and student success

A number of the proposals in the White Paper are likely to have a bearing on retention and student success. If implemented, some of their effects will be more direct than others.

More direct:

- Improved information for students;
- Restoring grants for students from lower-income families, and paying the first £1100 of their fees;
- Introducing a post-graduation income-contingent system of paying fees (in contrast to the existing system of 'up front' fee payments);
- Increased financial support for vulnerable students;
- Reimbursing institutions for the extra costs associated with enrolling students from disadvantaged backgrounds;
- Grant support for part-time students.

More indirect:

- Expansion of Foundation Degrees of two years full-time (or equivalent) duration;
- Encouragement of greater curricular flexibility, so that students can engage as suits their circumstances (though a corollary, from the institutional perspective, is that the performance indicator methodology needs to be more sensitive to intermittent engagement);
- Encouragement of good teaching in various ways;
- Benchmarking of institutional performance.

As one might expect, the proposals in the White Paper as a whole have had a mixed reception. The proposal for an 'Access Regulator' to monitor the access targets set by, and achievement of, institutions charging 'variable fees' has been subjected to criticism. Fierce debate continues regarding the most appropriate method of providing funding support for individuals and institutions. Likewise, there is debate as to whether a concentration on expansion of the system through Foundation Degrees is the most appropriate policy. The proposals for greater selectivity in research (which we have not considered here) have proved contentious.

The proposals have yet to complete their journey through the political process, and are likely to undergo some amendment in the light of political debate.

5

Institutional performance

Overview

Institutional statistics in respect of retention and completion rates are often perceived as 'hard' data, and they are used as such by some who have political axes to grind regarding their particular views of the contribution that higher education should be making to society. Those with a less partisan approach often look more carefully at the data that are presented. They try to get beneath them in order to understand why the data are as they are, and what signals and prompts the data send regarding the way higher education institutions go about their business. They realize that the data are 'softer' than they might appear at first sight. This chapter, therefore, offers a pinch of salt – maybe more – which readers may appreciate having to hand when looking at performance data.

Indicators in the international context

Performance indicators have for some time been sought in various countries as governments have tried to understand, and gain a measure of leverage over, national and state higher education systems. There has been a plethora of publications suggesting indicators, and there is little to be gained by reviewing what at times has seemed like a random walk through a jungle of possible measures, some of which have approached the edges of legality and sense. Krakower (1985) suggested, amongst 410 possible indicators, 'financial credit rating' and 'self-report of the effect of college attendance on alumni's personal body care'. Examples of the relatively early international interest in performance indicators include Dochy et al. (1990); Linke (1991); Ewell (1993); Kells (1990, 1993); JPIWG (1994a, 1994b) and Ruppert (1994).

The OECD indicators

Kells (1990, 1993) led the development of international compendia of indicator systems for the OECD. These early publications show that the thinking at that time in some of the contributor countries had not got much further than statements of principle. Practicable indicators were some way off, and the OECD took some years to develop a suite of system-level indicators in which it felt it could place reasonable confidence. 'Survival' rates (which are tantamount to completion rates in most instances) of students following 'Type A' programmes (typically first degree programmes) in higher education and graduation rates as percentages of the national population are given for selected countries in Table 5.1 (see: OECD 2000: 172–3, 2002: 46–7).

Technical details relating to the 2000 indicators can be found in OECD (2000: 344–7) and those relating to the 2002 indicators can be found in the OECD Technical Annex at *www.oecd.org/els/education/eag2002* (electronic publication only).

The difficulty with international comparisons is that the differences between national systems are obscured. Like is not necessarily being compared with like, as inspection of the technical commentary provided in OECD (2000: 344ff) clearly shows. If first degree programmes are taken as the focus of attention, then the length of these varies from country to country, but there is no obvious relationship between programme length and completion rate. Then, again, the way in which the data have been compiled varies: OECD's standard methodology – not used by all countries – uses a cross-section cohort (but some countries introduce weightings into the method); Denmark uses a 'synthetic' cohort; and the US and Finland use true cohort completion data. The US completion data includes students who are still on the institution's books after 5.5 years, which will underestimate non-completion since not all such students will go on to gain a first degree (OECD 2000: 345).

OECD statistics are necessarily based on national data sets, and are subject to the way that national systems compile and report data. UK data are, for example, projections of the completion rates that would occur for cohorts, assuming that the progression rates are those of previous cohorts. They are not actual completion rates. The data may, however, be the best that can be achieved in a reasonable time and hence be optimally useful for operational purposes. This is a particularly significant point where students may – as they tend to do in the US – take a considerable time to complete a programme of study.[38] Astin and Oseguera (2002: 7) showed, for example, that 57.6 per cent of their nationally representative sample of degree students in the US completed within six years, and that this figure crept upwards as the enrolment period increased. Sub-analyses showed that there was considerable variation between institutional types, and in respect of student backgrounds.

Table 5.1   Comparative 'survival' data for selected countries

	Survival rate, Year 1996*, all Type A first programmes (OECD 2000)	Tertiary graduation rate for all Type A first programmes, Year 1998 (OECD 2000)	Survival rate, Year 2000, all Type A first programmes (OECD 2002)	Tertiary graduation rate, all Type A first programmes, Year 2000 (OECD 2002)	Method of computation (see Notes)
Australia	65	25.8	69	36.3	1
Austria	53	13.7	59	16.0	2
Belgium (Flemish)	63	17.4	60		1
Czech Republic	79	28.4	61	27.9	1
Denmark	67		69	13.6	4
Finland	75	30.3	75	9.2	3
France	55	24.0	59	36.3	1
Germany	72	16.0	70	24.6	1
Hungary	77	24.7 +			2
Ireland	77	25.2 +	85	31.2	1
Italy	35	14.5	42	18.1	1
Japan	90	27.7 +	94	30.9	2
Mexico	68	10.1 +	69		1
The Netherlands	70	34.6	69		1
Portugal	49	17.5			1
Spain		27.9	77		
Sweden	74	25.1	48	28.1	1
Switzerland		20.1			
United Kingdom	81	35.2	83	37.5	2
United States	63	32.9	66	33.2	3

Notes

Type A programmes typically lead to degrees; Type B programmes typically do not.

* The reference years range between 1993 and 1997.

+ Other relevant data not included.

Blank cells indicate that data were not available.

Method of computation. 1: OECD standard methodology, cross-section cohort;

2: Cross-section cohort method (NB: UK used a weighted method);

3: True cohort method;

4: Synthetic cohort.

The reason for the discrepancy in the data from the Czech Republic is unclear.

A major factor bearing on completion is the nature of entering cohorts. A relatively open access approach to higher education is likely to lead to higher levels of non-completion than is a selective approach – Italy, for example, has high numbers in its entering cohorts, but expects the initial year to act as a 'natural' sifting mechanism and many students do not persist when they find themselves unable or unwilling to cope with the demands being made upon them. Added to this is the complication that in Italy young people can defer military service if they attend higher education, which is an attraction to students as far as entry is concerned, but a disadvantage to the nation when the students' non-completion is folded into the system's performance data (see Moortgat 1996).

The OECD statistics probably offer a reasonable representation of the ordering of nations as regards completion but, given the variation in data collection methodology, the actual 'survival' rates should not be taken as precise measures. They do not, of course, deal with the considerable intra-system variation in performance as exemplified in Australia by DEST (2001), in Ireland by Morgan et al. (2001), in the UK by HEFCE (2002), and in the US by Astin and Oseguera (2002).

Performance indicators in the UK

The Jarratt Report (CVCP 1985) examined efficiency in the UK university sector of that time. Of importance to this book are its initial suggestions regarding performance indicators, which were subsequently developed into 39 indicators (CVCP/UGC 1986), the set being enlarged to 69 by the mid-1990s (CVCP 1994). On the other side of the binary line, the Committee of Directors of Polytechnics (1987) was also grappling with the development of performance indicators, though it came up with a different emphasis in its recommendations, focusing on these institutions' successes in the light of a very different profile of student entry and research performance. The contemporaneous report[39] of the Good Management Practice Group of the National Advisory Body for Public Sector Higher Education (the body responsible at that time for allocating funding to polytechnics and colleges) included 'value added' as one of 14 indicators – an indicator which would attest to the gains made by students from their time in what was then labelled as 'the public sector of higher education' in contrast[40] to the universities. The intention was to make the political point that, even though the entry profile of students to this sector was less strong (as judged by traditional criteria), the performances of the graduating cohorts showed that students had benefited considerably from their time in higher education. 'Value added' was later examined in a report commissioned by the Council for National Academic Awards and the Polytechnics and Colleges Funding Council (CNAA/PCFC 1990), but the suggestions made came in for considerable criticism and, despite the superficial attractiveness of the concept, little progress has been made with this as an indicator because of technical problems with both the 'input' and 'output' measures.[41]

Retention and completion were not major issues for UK higher education at the time, though in the early 1990s the Joint Performance Indicators Working Group (JPIWG) was established with a brief to identify indicators that could be applied across the UK higher education sector. It produced a report (JPIWG 1994a) which was supplemented by a statistical commentary (JPIWG 1994b). During the 1990s, retention and completion indicators were placed firmly on the higher education agenda as successive governments sought better information regarding the sector's effectiveness. A report from a new Performance Indicators Working Group set up by the funding councils in the UK led to the publication of, first, a report on indicators (HEFCE 1999b) and, subsequently, a series of reports at roughly annual intervals (HEFCE 1999a, 2000, 2001a, 2002) which detailed aspects of institutional performance, including:

- Rates of non-completion following the first year of full-time undergraduate study;
- Projected completion rates for full-time undergraduates;
- Demographic data relating to participation (such as the proportions of entrants from 'working class' backgrounds, and of 'mature' entrants); and
- Employment following graduation.[42]

At the turn of the century, the Labour government made clear its intention to widen participation amongst those socio-economic groups whose level of participation languished well behind that of the middle class, thereby re-energizing the issue of access to higher education. However, this produced a marked tension between two policy concerns: on one hand, the government was concerned to minimize 'waste' in expenditure (here seen in terms of student non-completion, whose cost appeared non-trivial (Yorke 1999b)), yet on the other hand the institutional performance data that were produced demonstrated that those institutions most successful in attracting students from disadvantaged backgrounds tended to have high levels of student non-completion.

The national performance indicators for higher education published by HEFCE set institutional achievements in respect of retention and completion[43] for full-time study programmes against 'benchmarks' constructed by the Council's statisticians to take account of some of the variation in institutional characteristics[44] (such as 'subject mix') and the demographic characteristics of entering students.[45] The 'headline' statistics show marked variations between segments of the English higher education sector[46] (Table 5.2), which have been broadly stable over the four years of reporting.

The broad picture is clear. The old universities (that is, those that were designated as such prior to 1992) tend to have smaller proportions of students from lower socio-economic groups[47] and of 'mature' entrants,[48] and to have a higher incidence of students completing the programmes on

Table 5.2 Performance data in respect of full-time programmes in English higher education institutions. (Source: HEFCE 2002)

Institution type	N	Mean %	SD	Range
Percentage of entrants from socio-economic groups IIIm, IV and V				
Old university	43	20.0	6.0	9 to 35
New university	36	32.5	6.6	19 to 48
College (general)	14	32.8	5.2	26 to 45
Percentage of 'mature' entrants on first degree programmes				
Old university	43	12.3	7.8	4 to 34
New university	36	30.8	10.5	16 to 60
College (general)	14	29.4	9.1	14 to 50
Percentage non-completion (projected)				
Old university	43	9.6	5.3	1 to 29
New university	35	22.1	6.8	12 to 45
College (general)	13	17.0	6.2	11 to 30

Notes: Small and specialist institutions are excluded. For two institutions non-completion data were unavailable.

which they enrolled. Their entry is heavily dominated by school leavers with relatively good results in the Advanced Level examinations, a group that is biased towards the middle class.[49] The old universities are engaged to a much greater extent in research than are the other institutions. The new universities and the general colleges have a greater diversity of entrants and a lower incidence of completion. At the level of the whole-institution data, the relationship between the entry characteristics of students and non-completion is very strong (Yorke 2001a). The data for small and specialist institutions tend not to fit the general picture well, probably because of their particular characteristics.[50]

The robustness of indicators: the Linke investigations

A particularly thorough investigation of the robustness of indicators was led by the late Russell Linke in Australia (Linke 1991). The purpose of the study was to identify a set of performance indicators for Australian higher education institutions. The 'Linke Report' recommended 18 indicators as being suitable for national use, and supported each recommendation with a commentary on the robustness that could be expected in the indicator. The commentaries demonstrated that all of the indicators were to varying extents problematic, but that 18 were believed to be sufficiently robust for use by government. As Ewell and Jones (1994) put it:

> Many promising indicator systems fail simply because they are too expensive, too complex, too time-consuming, or too politically costly to

implement. Often the simplest is the best, even if it initially seems less technically attractive.

(Ewell and Jones 1994: 16)

The characteristics of indicators used by governments and agencies are, in other words, fairly rough and ready when compared with the technical qualities expected of research measures. The indicators recommended in the Linke Report are shown in Table 5.3.

Although a case can be made for a connection between retention/completion and some other of the Linke Report's indicators, the point that is of some interest here is that Linke and his colleagues felt able to recommend the student progress rate (that is, students' success in completing study units) but not the whole-programme completion rate – a matter to which we return in Chapter 10.

League tables and rankings

A brief mention needs to be made of institutional 'league tables' or 'rankings' since they are put before the public in the press and through books and magazine supplements that purport to offer guidance to intending students regarding the choice of higher education institution. The broadsheet press in the UK also publishes tables on an annual basis.

Whereas completion rates tend not to figure in these tables, some indexes that may bear on completion, such as student/staff ratios and library/learning resource expenditure, do. In analyses of early tables published by *The Times*, Yorke (1997, 1998b) showed that the overall rating of an institution correlated quite closely with research performance. Over the years there has been criticism of ranking or league tables on a variety of grounds (McGuire 1995; Morrison et al. 1995; Yorke 1997, 1998b; Bowden 2000), including the following:

- Dubious validity of some data (such as teaching quality assessments that have varied over time and across the different nations of the UK);
- Datedness of some data (such as those stemming from research assessment exercises, undertaken roughly quinquennially);
- High correlations between some of the measures used;
- Arbitrariness of the weightings given to the various indicators;
- Scoring methodology through which data are transformed to a common range;[51]
- Inappropriateness of some indicators (such as the proportion of foreign students);
- Combining of variables which are very different in kind; and
- Instability of some of the measures over time.

Even if one is prepared to give such tabulations the benefit of considerable doubt, they can at best only provide the broadest of depictions of what it is

Table 5.3 Performance indicators studied by Linke and his colleagues. (Those that were recommended for national use are shown in italics.)

Institutional context	Performance		Participation and social equity
	(a) In teaching and learning	**(b) In research and professional service**	
Equivalent full-time academic staff	Perceived teaching quality*	*Number of research grants*	*Academic staff gender ratio*
Academic support staff ratio	*Student progress rate*	*Value of research grants*	*Commencing student gender ratio*
Equivalent full-time student load	Programme completion rate	Average publication rate	Academic programme diversity
Student/staff ratio	Mean completion time	Productivity rate of other original works	
Student preference ratio	*Research higher degree productivity rate*	Paid consultancy rate	
Student application ratio	Graduate employment status	*Professional service activity*	
Student offer ratio			
Average student entry score			
Derivation of recurrent income			
Distribution of recurrent expenditure			
Academic activity cost per student			
Total recurrent cost per student			

*Data from the Course Experience Questionnaire (Ramsden 1991).

actually like to study a particular programme at a particular institution. There is no substitute for finding out at first hand what the student experience is likely to be. The more that students are expected to shoulder the burden of the costs of their higher education programmes, the more they are likely to make benefit/cost assessments of what is on offer, with the 'positional good' of having studied at a particular institution probably being a potent factor in their decision-making.

Surveys of graduate opinion

For some years the Graduate Careers Council of Australia (GCCA) has published the results of surveys of graduates regarding their experiences in higher education. These surveys are conducted some six months after graduation and constitute a retrospective view of graduates' perceptions of their courses using a variant of the Course Experience Questionnaire (CEQ) (Ramsden 1991). The findings are differentiated by subject discipline and institution, thus giving potential entrants to higher education what is purported to be a 'consumer's eye view' of relative strengths and weaknesses in an institution's provision. With an overall response rate of around 50 per cent, the results are probably as representative as can practically be achieved. The data appear in guides to choosing universities in Australia and hence have impact.

However, the interpretation of CEQ data is not as straightforward as might be supposed. The instrument[52] deals with aspects of higher education that are common to programmes across the sector, and hence cannot cater for programme-specific aspects of the higher education experience. Its items do not – and are not intended to – deal with the following:

- Specific curriculum content;
- Practical activities in laboratories, studios and the like;
- Provision of institutional facilities; and
- Course experiences that take place off-campus, such as in a workplace.

Further, the self-reporting of gain in 'generic' skills is likely to be affected by bias. An analogous survey under development for the UK seems likely to suffer from some similar difficulties, to judge from pilot work reported by Baty (2003).

Reading performance indicators

If league tables of institutions are of dubious value, what about the official indicator data published by HEFCE? These are authoritative, and as robust as can be achieved with the time and resources available to the funding councils. In Table 5.2 the differences between categories of institution are readily apparent. The tables of demographic variables show that some institutions succeed in 'beating their benchmarks' even when demographic data suggest that this will be particularly challenging. Chapter 9 follows this through in terms of what some institutions are doing to support student success.

Headline retention and completion rates are seductive. Elite universities tend to do considerably better than others on these indicators because their entrants

- Generally have high A-level scores;
- Are aged around 18;
- Are more likely to be middle class;

and hence are more likely to possess

- The cultural and social capital that are supportive of success;
- Sources of financial support that are less available to those from lower socio-economic groups; and
- Less fear of debt than students from disadvantaged backgrounds.

To this picture must be added the approach adopted by particular groups – for example, Muslim students are more debt-averse than most because of religious considerations. Some groups of students are not dispersed evenly across the higher education sector, with implications of disproportionate effects on institutional performance.

The demographic data show that the new universities and general colleges tend to attract older students and proportionately more students from disadvantaged backgrounds, whose characteristics tend to be the obverse of those listed in respect of elite universities. In some specialist subject areas, such as Art and Design, the new universities and colleges have strong traditions which have led them to be the main providers, and hence the general pattern regarding enrolments is not followed. It should also be noted that a few of the older universities have profiles of performance and student demographics that are quite like those of new universities, but they are set apart by their generally higher profiles in research.

Press coverage of the UK performance indicators for higher education[53]

The first set of national data that were published in 1999 stimulated a considerable amount of attention in both the broadsheet and (to a lesser extent) the tabloid press. Prominent in the coverage was the cost to the nation's finances of non-completion, which the minister of the day construed as 'a waste of talent'. Institutions were named and shamed, or praised according to their completion figures. Highly selective institutions were shown to have high levels of completion; the less selective to have lower levels of completion. These data, whose general tenor was well known in the sector (see the last section of Table 5.2), confirmed that the more an institution enrolled students from disadvantaged backgrounds of various kinds, the greater was the incidence of (projected) non-completion.

The coverage in the press, not surprisingly, reflected the general ideological stance of the newspaper. The right-wing press lambasted a number of new universities for their relatively low levels of non-completion under colourful headlines like 'Shocking waste of the student dropouts' (*The Daily Mail*) and 'Hard-up university dropouts who shame our nation' (*The Express*), though the latter did acknowledge a contributory factor – that of the weaker economic position of entrants from disadvantaged backgrounds. A subsidiary theme was criticism of the governmental policy of widening access to higher education. *The Daily Mail* took the opportunity to print an article which questioned the ability of some students to study at higher education level. Other newspapers took a more balanced line, noting that there was an unevenness between institutions as regards the class-profile of their entrants which needed to be set against the published completion data.

The publication of the data gave some an opportunity to score political points. Some of the point-scoring was manifestly unfair. For example, Scottish Nationalist and Conservative politicians laid the blame for poor completion in Scotland on the Labour government's introduction of tuition fees and the phasing-out of the maintenance award in favour of a loan system, conveniently overlooking the fact that the data predated these changes, and were really attributable to the final stages of the preceding UK Conservative administration.

In the summer of 2000 the so-called 'Laura Spence affair' erupted into public awareness. Laura Spence was a pupil from a state school who had obtained an excellent set of passes at Advanced Level but had been rejected for a place at Magdalen College, Oxford. This created a political furore that focused attention more sharply on access (especially to elite universities), which became a 'hot topic' in the press for a while. This affair seems to have influenced the tone of the press reportage of the performance data from 2000 onwards, though the general level of engagement has been lower than for the first publication, probably because the novelty value has disappeared and, in any case, the shifts in institutional performance figures tend to be relatively small (after all, the nature of higher education militates against rapid change in performance data). From the point of view of a press which tends to favour the dramatic, a headline such as 'Not much change' has little allure.

Following the 'Laura Spence affair', there was a turnaround in the relative prominences of non-completion and access, with the latter now being the dominant theme in the press. The comparison of coverage in 2000 with that of 1999 illustrates how the focus of emphasis had shifted. All of the headlines in the national daily press in 2000 focused on elitism and class, whereas in the previous year they contained only a few oblique allusions. In some newspapers the elite institutions, praised for completion rates in the previous year, were criticized for the bias in their intakes against students from working class backgrounds. The relatively low completion rates in some institutions were still the subject of comment, but this now tended to be related to the demographic background of entrants.

Since 2000 the press treatment of the performance data has not had a consistent theme. There has been a tendency amongst the tabloid press to revert to the 'shock, horror' reporting of high non-completion rates, with the facts not being allowed to intrude too much on a good story. Though the proportion of UK students projected not to gain a qualification has been steady to a percentage point since the 1999 publication (and was 16 per cent in 2002), this did not prevent *The Daily Mail* from excitedly headlining its 2001 reporting with 'College drop-outs soar' or *The Mirror* misleadingly declaring 'Crisis as 41% uni students drop out' (a figure that related to a single institution in London which serves an area of considerable disadvantage).

What the institutional performance data cannot tell government and agencies

Although the data published by HEFCE are undoubtedly of high quality, they do not fully illuminate the retention/completion picture. They do not differentiate between student departures that could (at least in part) be attributed to institutionally-related causes and those that arise from the students' own life-style choices or from extraneous events. The research undertaken in the north-west of England by Yorke and colleagues (Yorke et al. 1997; Yorke 1999b) showed that some students left their programmes because they felt that the institution concerned had let them down in some way. It also showed that others had left their programmes because, for example, they had failed to adjust to a new-found freedom or they had become irredeemably worried by debt.

If the interest is in the performance of *institutions*, then a question has to be raised regarding the use of statistical methods that do not 'partial out' departures that derive from events beyond an institution's control. Such departures are likely to be unevenly spread throughout the higher education system. For example, institutions enrolling higher proportions of students from relatively disadvantaged circumstances are likely to suffer disproportionately from withdrawals stimulated by debt or fear of debt.[54] Other correlates of class, such as poorer health and difficulty in affording childcare, are similarly likely to be disproportionated across the higher education system.

'Per year' and 'per programme' (non-)completion statistics are unable to take account of departures that derive from non-institutional causes. In Australia, the Student Progress Unit (SPU) is used as the index of student success (Dobson et al. 1996): its analogues in the UK would be the proportion of modules passed or credits attained by students. These are preferable as an indicator of the degree of success attained by the *partnership of student and institution*, for the following reasons:

- They eliminate withdrawals between study units (modules) and between years that are caused by events beyond the institution's control.

(They cannot, of course, eliminate the effects of such causes during study units.)

- They should focus institutional attention on study units for which success rates are unduly low (or perhaps, and from a different point of view, unduly high) and hence encourage appropriate and focused enhancement activity.
- They enable part-time and full-time study to be treated on the same basis, as far as student success is concerned. At present, the national statistics reflect a view of higher education that is centred on full-time and sandwich[55] study. Part-time study is recognized only in the publication of module success rates for Welsh institutions.

The sophistication of contemporary data management systems makes feasible such an approach to institutional performance assessment.

There are further considerations. First, in the UK there has been a tendency to encourage students to enrol for the highest award for which their qualifications make them eligible, since registration is then a 'once only' cost. Some students may not intend to complete a degree programme: instead they may envisage 'stepping off' with an intermediate award. However, enrolment for the highest award keeps options open at no cost to the student, and so a departure with an intermediate award can be – from the student's point of view – the intended success, whereas from the institution's perspective (and from that of the national completion statistics) it counts as a non-completion. A similar argument can be deployed in respect of the student who leaves higher education to take up an appropriate employment opportunity (as, until the recent international economic downturn, was particularly likely to be the case for those with expertise in computing).

Second, the pattern of student engagement in higher education in the UK is evolving towards that of the US, with students combining study and employment in various proportions. Some may choose to take more than one year out of higher education (the limit of the current national computations regarding completion) in order to replenish personal finances, to commit to childcare, or to undertake some other form of enrichment such as voluntary service. A realistic perspective on completion needs to take this into account. Lifelong learning was a political mantra of a few years ago, and a more relaxed view of completion is consistent with the notion. However, political attention has shifted to the widening of participation and graduate employability, and hence there is less political 'push' to move the indexing of completion further on.

What the data cannot tell intending students

The indicators provide an overview of institutional performance that is valuable to managers as they respond to various initiatives and expectations.

They are less use to a lay readership because of the difficulty of decoding what they portend for someone who might want to join an institution, or who is seeking to provide a potential entrant with advice. In themselves the indicators offer little by way of suggesting what the quality of the student experience might be like. There is a risk of choosing the 'wrong' institution by focusing on its reputation and not on the nature of the course it is offering.

Some students are more at home in one kind of institutional environment than another. This may be due to perceptions of a class differential: Forsyth and Furlong (2003) provide examples of students from disadvantaged backgrounds in Scotland who found a formidable class barrier in the elite institutions in which they had enrolled. The class divide works both ways, since middle class students can be uncomfortable in institutions that they construe as serving a working class population.

The difficulties experienced by some students may, however, be related to age or culture, rather than class, or to a complex interaction between factors such as these.

What the data can tell institutional managers

Retention and completion statistics allow institutions to judge their performances against those of other institutions which they see as being comparable, and the computation of 'benchmarks' that allow for some demographic variables exposes to view particularly strong or weak performances. The HEFCE statistics are at whole-institutional level, but data from internal student record systems are available at various levels of disaggregation. Intra-institutional analyses are then able to pinpoint departments or programmes that exhibit particularly strong or weak performances, so that managers can inquire as to the causes (such as differences in intakes) and instigate action where appropriate.[56]

A number of institutions have looked at the first year of their programmes, which is where around two-thirds of withdrawals are found. Many modular schemes included summative assessment at the end of the first semester (around Christmas). Failures and weak performances tend to prompt withdrawal either immediately, or after a stressful period of 'failing and trailing' modules. From a pedagogic point of view, bearing in mind that many students may take longer than a single semester to come to terms with the demands of higher education, and also to settle into the institutional culture, such early summative assessments are counter-productive – particularly when the first year as a whole is usually a qualifying year for honours-level study, and merely has to be passed. The publication of retention data has refocused institutional attention on the educational purpose of the first year of full-time study.

Napier University has been particularly successful in improving its whole-institution retention and completion rates (Table 5.4), by focusing on the

Table 5.4   Performance data for Napier University (Sources: Table 3a, all entrants in HEFCE 1999a, 2000, 2001a, 2002)

Year of entry	Percentage not continuing in higher education following year of entry			
	1996–97	1997–98	1998–99	1999–2000
% not continuing	19	8	11	8
Benchmark	12	12	13	14

first year experience (where the loss of students is the greatest). According to Johnston (2003) there was at the outset no institutional 'master plan' for the improvement of retention. The Student Retention Project that began in 1994 set in motion a series of actions embracing research, sharing findings and promoting improved practices whose effect on institutional performance can be inferred from the institutional data relating to continuation after the first year of full-time study. The actions taken by the university included

• Providing reliable data;
• Keeping retention visible in the university;
• Encouraging reflection on retention-related issues during the monitoring and evaluation of academic offerings;
• Supporting staff through workshops and consultancy;
• Encouraging the review of approaches to teaching, learning and assessment;
• Setting pass-rate targets for all years of undergraduate degrees, as part of a general commitment to continual improvement; and
• Applauding successes.

Summing up

Retention, 'survival' and completion are three indicators that are often used in assessing institutional performance. This brief survey has shown that, whatever the level of engagement, these parameters need to be treated with caution lest – as the tabloid press in the UK graphically evidences – misleading inferences are drawn. Used wisely, indicators can help institutional managers to focus on aspects of provision that might benefit from some form of enhancement activity. If this happens (and some suggestions to that end are offered in Chapter 10), then both students and institutional performance should benefit.

6

Theory: a multiplicity of perspectives

Overview

The wide variety of influences on students as they progress through higher education suggests that appeal needs to be made to a similarly wide range of theoretical constructs if a satisfactory theory of retention and success (or their obverse, attrition and failure) is to be constructed. The theoretical formulations in the literature relating to retention have been influenced by both psychology and sociology, the balance between the two reflecting the theorists' backgrounds and predilections.

We argue in this chapter that the theoretical net has not been cast wide enough to deal with the manifold ways in which students can be influenced to stay in higher education and succeed or to leave higher education either temporarily or permanently. A consequence of our reflections on theory is that, as has been the case in sociology, the quest for 'grand theory' is unlikely to meet with success.

Theoretical pluralism

Interest in student retention and student persistence at university level education has been sustained over a period in excess of fifty years in the US. Braxton (2000b: 1) notes that the 'departure puzzle' has been around for over seventy years and cites reviews by Summerskill in 1962 and Pantage and Creedon in 1978 which, he claims, mark 'the longevity of this line of inquiry'. The bulk of attempts to understand retention and persistence originate from the US. Stage and Anaya (1996) point out, however, that much of the current understanding of student retention has relied on causal modelling research most frequently centred on white, middle class, young American freshers in private, residential institutions. Given this particular socio-demographic background, it is risky to extrapolate from it to a wider student population which includes ethnically diverse and older students, some studying on a part-time basis and/or commuting from home to the institution.

A variety of theoretical constructs has relevance for student success, though theorists of different inclination regarding retention have concentrated their attention on particular aspects. The theoretical literature on retention has drawn inspiration from a range of disciplines – psychology (for example Bean and Eaton 2000), sociology (for example Tinto 1993) and organizational behaviour (for example Bean and Metzner 1985) – though in no case can it be convincingly argued that the theoretical formulations that have been produced are monodisciplinary in character. Astin's (1991) I-E-O [input-environment-output] model, though based on psychological constructs and behaviour, has affinities with economics. Cabrera et al. (1992) explicitly fused the Tinto model with that of Bean and Metzner (1985), and Sandler (2000) extended the fused model in order to take better account of the circumstances of older students. In this chapter we concentrate on the two main disciplines involved, sociology and psychology.

Sociology or psychology?

The early literature, which was American in origin, tended to have a bias towards sociology, reflecting the pioneering work of Spady (1970) and its development by Tinto (1975). Spady's and Tinto's work filled a vacuum in a field of research that had been devoid of a conceptual framework. Tinto's work, developed over a considerable time, has been very influential in studies of retention and attrition. Some have seen it primarily in sociological terms, but his basic model implies psychology in components such as intentions, goals and commitments and, of course, the decision whether to depart from, or stay in, higher education.

Reviewing theories and models of student development and college impact, Pascarella and Terenzini (1991: 57–8) point out that, where college impact is concerned, the emphasis is on the college environment as an 'active force' operating on students. They suggest that developmental theorizing also needs to be brought into consideration if a more rounded approach is to be adopted to student-institution interaction and its outcomes. One problem for today's theoretically inclined researcher is that most of the developmental theorists mentioned by Pascarella and Terenzini have faded from the forefront of attention. A second is that, for many students (especially commuter students, who often attend institutions on a part-time basis), events outside college may have a considerable bearing on their persistence in studying. Tinto makes his position on the psychological perspective very clear:

> However framed, all these [psychological] views of departure share a
> common theme, namely that retention and departure are primarily the

reflection of individual actions and therefore are largely due to the ability or willingness of the individual to successfully complete the tasks associated with college attendance. More important, such models invariably see student departure as reflecting some shortcoming and/ or weakness in the individual.

(Tinto 1993: 85)

Tinto goes on to suggest that, if the psychological perspective were important, attrition could be reduced by actions such as improving students' learning skills and/or enrolling only those who have appropriate personality traits. Whilst he acknowledges that there is a correlation between the selectivity of an institution and retention (which data from Astin and Oseguera (2002) confirm) many US institutions do not have the luxury of being able to select their student bodies.

The difficulty with the psychological view of departure, according to Tinto, is that

...it is not truly explanatory nor well suited to the policy needs of most colleges. [...] Though it does point up the necessary role of personality in individual responses to educational situations, this perspective has not yet been able to tell us why it is that some personality attributes appear to describe differences among stayers and leavers in some situations but not in others.

(Tinto 1993: 86)

Tinto's perspective is implicitly that of the institution seeking to optimize student retention and success,[57] and this is consistent with our intentions in writing this book. However, the psychological literature on which he draws is relatively limited, and it is surely inappropriate to charge psychological theorizing with seeing departure in terms of student weakness or failure, which comes close to 'blaming the victim': after all, his own theory can be seen in terms of the student applying a rational calculus of the relative advantages of staying or leaving. Would Tinto see a student leaving higher education to take up a good job as exhibiting weakness or failure, for example? (Naïve performance statistics might have it so.) Further, Tinto appears not to address how the institution might change the *psychological* context in order to increase the chances of student success. The psychological perspective, we argue, offers more than Tinto seems prepared to allow.

Our position is that retention and student success are influenced by a complex set of considerations which are primarily psychological and sociological, but which are in some cases influenced by matters that might be located under other disciplinary banners such as that of economics. Student persistence and withdrawal are often, but not always, matters of personal decision (or, in some cases, the kind of 'non-decision' that characterizes drift) and are, at root, psychologically grounded. However, the treatment of students in[58] a higher education institution and broader societal pressures may well exert determining influence.

If the quality of the student experience plays a part in student departure, as Yorke's (1999a) findings suggest, then the approach taken by an institution may support students or undermine them. Tinto's (1993) point that psychological models are insufficient is well made, and he points towards the need to engage with sociological theorizing. Once the sociological is brought into play, then student departure is the outcome of transactions between student and institution (and student and student), in which a breakdown can be interpreted from the perspective of either party. The psychologically-based perspective does not require that the 'blame' for withdrawal be attached to the student – it simply makes it more difficult for other possible interpretations to be admitted into consideration.

Sociological perspectives

Tinto's theory of individual departure

Over a period of two decades Tinto (1975, 1987, 1993) has developed a longitudinal interactionist model of student departure which has been adopted widely by the research community as a basis from which to work. The idea of transition from one culture to another is central to his approach, which draws to a considerable extent on two main sources of inspiration: first, Durkheim's (1951) theory of suicide and, later on, van Gennep's (1908) study of rites of passage. The reader is referred to Tinto (1993) for an elaboration. Tinto's theory suggests that students who decide to leave early have found that the process of adopting the new social values too difficult: they have not managed to integrate into the institution, academically and/or socially. He follows this up by arguing that institutions carry much of the responsibility for the failure of students because of their unwillingness or inability to make appropriate accommodations.

From his anthropological perspective, Tierney (1992, 2000), sees Tinto's approach to transition as flawed. In his article of 1992, he advanced four points of criticism:

- The basis for Tinto's notion of ritual, van Gennep's 'rite of passage', is intra-cultural and was never intended to refer to the passage of an individual from one culture to another.
- Participation in, and departure from, a ritual are not matters of personal choice, since ritual is governed by the culture.
- Relatedly, in Tinto's theory the focus is on college attendance as an individual matter, which goes against the use of cultural theorizing.
- There is a failure to acknowledge that Tinto brings a nativist or insider's perspective to 'native rituals'.

Our view is that the notion of a unidirectional transition is inadequate. As Tierney argues with respect to native Americans, students with no familial background of higher education do not necessarily abandon their home environment; they are more likely to expand their world-view to encompass their new experiences. If, though, they find themselves unable to make such an accommodation (as students with boyfriends or girlfriends at home sometimes do), and/or perceive the higher educational environment as unwelcoming, then – as we shall see in Chapter 8 – they may decide to leave.

Tinto (1993: 106ff) distinguishes between the academic and social systems in an institution, seeing them as separate yet interconnected. Persistence is dependent on an adequate level in the academic system but, with possible exceptions such as outstanding athletes, success in the social system is insufficient. A student may be integrated in one system but not the other. Commuter and part-time students may not, for various reasons, become integrated socially, and be relatively isolated from peer support.

Many researchers have used Tinto's theorizing as the basis for their work on retention and departure. However, the broadness of the constructs creates problems regarding the consistency of their use. Kuh and Love (2000: 197) implicitly illustrate the point when they say:

> Academic integration represents the extent to which students are doing reasonably well in their classes (academic achievement), perceive their classes to be relevant and have practical value (e.g., prepare them for jobs), and are satisfied with their majors. Social integration refers to students' levels of social and psychological comfort with their colleges' milieus, association with or acceptance by affinity groups, and sense of belonging that provides the security needed to join with others in common causes, whether intellectual or social.

Braxton and Lien (2000) point to problems with the specification of 'academic integration', as far as measurement of its effects is concerned. Further, Braxton (2000a: 258), reflecting on the parts of Tinto's theory that are most strongly supported (those relating to social integration: see the following chapter), remarks that 'social integration remains unexplained'.

It is not surprising to find academic and social integration being interpreted and operationalized in different ways, which means that the cumulation of research findings is more problematic than might appear at first sight.

In his book, Braxton (2000a) discusses whether Tinto's theory should be discarded because of its weaknesses, or further developed. In the following chapter, Braxton and Hirshy show that, whereas some aspects of Tinto's model that relate to social integration have obtained a substantial measure of empirical support, others have not. Braxton's (2000a) view is that, on balance, it is preferable to work with a theoretical approach that has had some empirical success than to start on a new theoretical journey.

Bourdieu's theory of social reproduction

Bourdieu's sociological theorizing (Bourdieu 1973; Bourdieu and Passeron 1977) has recently entered the literature on retention in the US (McDonough 1994, 1997; Berger 2000) and the UK (Longden 2002a; Thomas 2002; Yorke and Thomas 2003). Bourdieu (1973) developed the idea of 'cultural capital' to provide an explanation for social inequalities. 'Cultural capital' refers to the cultural resources possessed by people, striking an analogy with the possession of financial resources. Some students are well endowed with cultural capital; others are not. The former will have acquired understandings of what is expected in particular environments, often as a matter of course,[59] whereas the latter have not had the same kind of exposure (see Grenfell and James 1998 on this point).

Individuals who can access the various sources of capital constitute the dominant class and are able to use their resources to maintain their position relative to others. Following Bourdieu, McDonough (1997) has argued that cultural capital has no intrinsic value other than the way it can be converted, manipulated, and invested in other forms of highly prized resources, including economic capital. She argues that it is a type of knowledge that those in the upper class value but that it is not taught in formal schooling. McDonough (1994) also argued that social class is a major shaping force. Students from the higher socio-economic groups have a narrow range of appropriate higher education institutions (that is, the highly selective and prestigious) from which to make their selection if they want to maintain or improve their economic and social status. In contrast, students from lower socio-economic groups are less likely to believe they are entitled to university education, especially in the most prestigious institutions (Archer and Hutchings 2000; Archer et al. 2003). However, some students are enabled by the higher education system to increase their stock of cultural capital (Grenfell and James 1998; Schuller 2000): the poor student enabled to succeed at a 'top' university through a scholarship or grant epitomizes this.

Bourdieu's concept of 'habitus', which can be summarized as the collectivity of norms and practices of a social group, points towards the problems that are faced by students who find themselves in an unfamiliar environment: there is a mismatch between the student and group as regards habitus, and success is likely to depend upon the extent to which this can be reduced. Thus, in the educational arena, successful navigation of a system of higher education that is inherently elite requires prior familiarity with elite cultural codes: students who are unfamiliar with these codes find it difficult to achieve educational success. The disjunction between the culture of the home environment and the culture of the university makes it more difficult for students from poor backgrounds to integrate and persist in higher education: the point is consistent with Tinto's discussion of the importance of social integration. The educational system discriminates, implicitly if not explicitly, against students from non-elite cultures because the transition from home to university is harder for them to complete.

Berger (2000) makes the point that, while the main focus in the USA has been on socio-demographic characteristics, in order to understand persistence from a social reproduction perspective it is necessary to

> consider the issue of access to various capital resources ... [because] there has been no research on the effects of students' initial levels of cultural capital on retention.
>
> (Berger 2000: 113)

Berger (2000: 113ff) identifies four main propositions that could be topics for research:

1. Institutions with higher levels of cultural capital will have the highest retention rates.
2. Students with higher levels of cultural capital are more likely to persist, across all types of institutions, than are students with less access to cultural capital.
3. Students with higher levels of cultural capital are most likely to persist at institutions with correspondingly high levels of organizational cultural capital
4. Students with access to lower levels of cultural capital are more likely to persist at institutions with correspondingly low levels of organizational cultural capital.

Whilst Berger may be correct regarding the absence of research explicitly relating cultural capital to retention, circumstantial evidence from Astin and Oseguera (2002) in the US and the various sets of institutional performance statistics produced in the UK by HEFCE (for example, HEFCE 2002) suggest that the level of cultural capital is associated with retention and success; that is that the first proposition is supported. Whilst it might be speculated that the relationship is causal, any such causality will be heavily mediated. Evidence collected by Astin et al. (1996) and Astin and Oseguera (2002) suggests that the second proposition may be true. Whilst the remaining two propositions are intuitively plausible, the ambiguity introduced into each by the lack of a comparator is unhelpful. There is some limited evidence from Finland (Liljander 1998) that 'trading up' to a more prestigious programme or 'trading down' to a less prestigious programme is associated with class, which would be consistent with Berger's propositions.

Psychological perspectives

Bean and Eaton (2000) suggest that, because Tinto's (1975, 1993) sociologically-oriented research has dominated the development of concepts relating to student retention, the contribution of psychological theories has been less well developed.

Bean and Eaton (2000) review psychological theories related to student retention, and identify four dominant theories that they regard as useful for research on retention:

- Attitude-behaviour theory, linking beliefs, attitudes and intentions with behaviour;
- Coping behaviour theory, which can be seen in terms of adjustment to, or 'fit' with, an environment;
- Self-efficacy – in essence, the individual's perception that they can act to achieve a desired outcome; and
- Attribution theory, where the key issue is the extent to which control is possessed by the individual, or is believed to lie outside their control. Rotter's (1966) construct of 'locus of control' is of key importance.

The model that they propose suggests that students enter college with a complex set of characteristics and traits and that during their various interactions with the institution aspects of their psychological state undergo change.[60] Where the change is positive, the student experiences an increased sense of self-efficacy, reduced stress, increased confidence and a greater sense of personal control, which leads through various iterative processes via academic and social integration, and commitment to the institution, ultimately to persistence. Bean and Eaton believe that it copes with Tinto's criticism that psychological theory contributes solely to involuntary early departure and says little about voluntary departure. They acknowledge that their model has a fuzziness that derives from the inability to deal in detail with the various contributing theories to which they appeal.

More psychological theories can be brought to bear on retention and success than are cited by Bean and Eaton. We suggest that those listed below are worthy of consideration:

- Motivation (Pintrich and Schunk 1996);
- Self-efficacy (Bandura 1997), which is acknowledged by Bean and Eaton: in broad terms, the belief that one can achieve success if effort is put in. Associated with this is an optimistic approach to life (Seligman 1998) and an internal locus of control (Rotter 1966);
- 'Malleable' self-theorizing (Dweck 1999), as compared with 'fixed' self-theorizing;
- 'Practical intelligence' (Sternberg 1997);
- Emotional intelligence (Goleman 1996, following Salovey and Mayer 1990);
- The adoption of learning goals rather than goals relating to one's performance vis-à-vis that of others (Dweck 1999); and
- Constructivism in learning and teaching, which has a long academic pedigree and has latterly been promoted by Biggs (for example Biggs 2003), amongst others.

All of these are likely to bear on a student's persistence in higher education, especially when the going gets hard. Self-evidently, if a student is not particularly motivated as regards their programme (for example, because of having made an ill-considered choice), then their persistence and success are at risk. Connected with motivation is a set of constructs related to a student's sense of agency – whether they believe that they can 'make a difference' in what they do;[61] how strongly they feel they are in control of what they are doing (as opposed to feeling that they are – to put it colourfully – victims of circumstance); and whether they see aspects of their 'self' as open to development or as 'givens' within whose limits they have to operate. The last of these is exemplified by 'intelligence'. Yorke and Knight (2004) found that, of more than 2000 first and final year students in programmes across four varied institutions, two in seven appeared to take the view that their intelligence was fixed rather than mutable. In other words, these students could be implicitly imposing a limit on what they envisage themselves achieving.

Sternberg (1997) has argued that weight needs to be given to 'practical intelligence' as well as to 'academic intelligence': the most academically intelligent are not necessarily the most successful. Further, Sternberg and Grigorenko (2000) indicate that practical intelligence can grow throughout life (another way of asserting the value of experiential learning), whereas academic intelligence may gently decline from early adulthood. Whilst Sternberg's perspective has relevance for all students, it is probably particularly significant for students entering higher education with relatively modest qualifications and/or as 'second chance' students following a period of employment or caring responsibility. Such students may have a fairly fragile self-belief regarding their capacity to succeed in their studies and, if teachers are insensitive to their need for encouragement (or, worse, preemptively dismiss their potential), they may be discouraged to the extent that they withdraw.

With success in higher education being increasingly tied to the expectations of the labour market, emotional intelligence – important in respect of students' experience in higher education – gains further significance, especially in respect of the ability to contribute to an employment environment. Awareness of self and of others, the capacity to express oneself and relate constructively to others, to exercise self-control even at times of high emotion, and to cope with the various challenges that life throws up, all have a part to play in student success – though how much of a part will depend on the extent to which the pedagogic approaches adopted encourage their development.

Whilst Tinto (1993: 132–3) acknowledges that the classroom comprises a social system and can provide social engagements that would otherwise be unavailable to many students who attend on a commuter basis, he glosses over the important role that pedagogy can play in developing a student's sense of engagement.[62] Pascarella and Terenzini (1991: 94ff, 146–7) concluded that student gain in subject disciplinary learning and in general cognitive development was influenced by the way in which teachers went about their task.

Success is likely to be influenced by the approach that students adopt in respect of their learning. The distinction between deep and surface learning first made by Marton and Säljö (1976) is well-embedded in the literature of pedagogy in higher education, with the benefits of deep learning being promoted. Prosser and Trigwell (1999), for example, draw attention to the importance of approaches to teaching, and the need for teaching to encourage students to adopt deep, rather than surface, approaches to learning. Dweck (1999) distinguishes between 'learning' and 'performance' goals,[63] which adds a further dimension. The student whose primary motivation is to keep up appearances (or, in other terms, bolster the self) is likely to find failure relative to their peers discouraging; in contrast, the student whose psychological orientation is towards learning is likely to see failure as an opportunity for further learning. As Rogers (2002) points out, learning is not free from risk. Yet curricular structures often implicitly discourage the taking of risks in learning: students pick up the 'message' that they should attain and maintain high grades on modules because their final grade-point average or honours degree classification depends upon the cumulation of grades. There is an implicit pressure to 'play safe', and to perform with a desired grade in mind.

A way of thinking

The sheer complexity of the range of influences on students makes the further development of theories of student retention or success a more heroic undertaking than we are prepared to attempt here. Indeed, we remain unconvinced that a single theoretical formulation – a 'grand theory' – can be constructed to include all of the possible influences that bear, via the student's psychological state, on retention and success, whilst being practicable in terms of research and institutional practice. Hence a comprehensive predictive theory is probably beyond reach. The same probably holds for an explanatory theory, though it is feasible to appeal to the variety of extant theories to which we have alluded (and others) in order to seek greater understanding of the ways in which student departure, retention and success are influenced.

Figure 6.1 is our attempt to schematize in the broadest of terms the layered set of influences on student departure. We place the student's individual psychology at the heart of decision-making as to whether to persist or leave, but the outer two layers acknowledge that the contexts of the institution and the broader social environment exert their influence on the student.[64] The outer two layers should not be taken as implying that societal influences on the individual's psychological state are mediated by the institutional context, since many such influences will have direct impact.

Our purpose here is limited to suggesting a *general way of thinking* about the retention issue. Like all schematizations of this sort, the Figure grossly

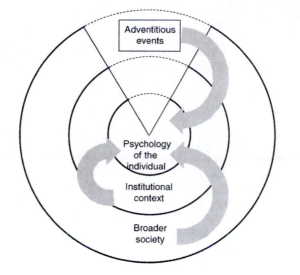

Figure 6.1 A schematization of the influences on the student's psychological state

oversimplifies what is obviously a very complex set of social and psychological interactions.

In this chapter we have, therefore, indicated a range of possible influences on the trajectories of students through higher education and suggest that, whilst some influences may be sufficient on their own to precipitate withdrawal, the chances of withdrawal are higher the greater the number of them that impinge negatively on a student's experience. For some students, a single influence may be sufficiently powerful on its own to precipitate departure: on occasion, the decision regarding departure will be beyond the student's control, such as when they are the victim of an accident or suffer from health-related problems. Exclusion because of academic failure (involuntary departure) is difficult to interpret in the abstract since it could stem from a variety of causes, ranging from excesses in a student's social life – a matter of student control (or, more accurately, its lack) – to weaknesses in the learning experience (perhaps a matter relating to institutional provision): without an understanding of the prevailing conditions one cannot tell.

Developing an understanding of departure and success

There are two main approaches to the development of understanding about departure, retention and success, quantitative and qualitative. Each has advantages and disadvantages.

Quantitative approaches

Quantitative approaches appear in two commonly employed forms. The first form involves the analysis of datasets in order to identify correlates of student behaviour. National or state policy makers and institutions value this kind of work since it provides them with data that have the 'massness' that enables them to understand in broad terms how the system or institution is performing and thus helps them make policy decisions at the 'macro' level designed to improve the effectiveness and efficiency of the system or institution. Some examples are the analyses carried out by Astin et al. (1996) and Astin and Oseguera (2002) on student graduation in the US; the institutional performance statistics produced in the UK by HEFCE; and the quantitative aspects of the 'autopsy' studies of withdrawn students conducted in England by Yorke (1999b) and Davies and Elias (2003).

The second form consists of the testing of theoretical models (which are often quite complex) by combining results from standard inventories and other experimental measures with demographic data. The results are critically dependent on a number of considerations, including the sample of students (the strictures of Stage and Anaya (1996) are relevant here); the validity of the instrumentation; the reliability with which the instruments measure the intended constructs; the response rate; and the percentage of the variance in the dependent variable(s) explained by the model. Some complex path analyses using a plethora of independent variables (implicitly presumed not to be highly correlated[65]) may explain only relatively low proportions of the variance in retention, suggesting strongly that persistence and retention are much more complex constructs than the research model was able to capture. Such findings also point to the challenge faced by those who wish to theorize the topic. For instance, an analysis of data from Bowling Green State University showed that a complex set of variables accounted for 33 per cent of the variance in student retention: the authors of this report compared this figure favourably with others[66] in which the variance explained was around half this value (Office of Institutional Research – BGSU 2001). Other examples of this general (and widely used) approach can be found in Cabrera et al. (1992), Sandler (2000) and Thomas (2000).

Qualitative approaches

Qualitative approaches are strongly oriented to increasing an understanding of the phenomena of departure, persistence and success. Rarely are there the resources to conduct qualitative studies on a large scale. A notable large-scale qualitative study was conducted in the US by Seymour and Hewitt (1997). They used a mixture of individual interviews and focus group discussions with 460 students of science, mathematics and engineering in order to gain an understanding of why some students switched from these subjects during their time in higher education whilst others persisted (some, it turned out, in environments inimical to learning). The qualitative approach is more prominent in research in the UK (reflecting not only the dominant approach to educational research in that country but also perhaps in recognition that cohort numbers are often smaller than in US institutions). Qualitative methodology is evident in studies by Longden (2001b), Reay (2001) and Read et al. (2003). It is also present, though only to a limited extent, in the studies reported by Yorke (1999b) and Davies and Elias (2003), whose quantitative 'autopsy' surveys were supplemented with opportunities for ex-students to elaborate on standardized response categories.

Is there a methodological 'best buy'?

There is no methodological 'best buy' for all purposes. The research question (sociological, psychological, or other) must determine the most appropriate line of inquiry, and the research method then needs to be rigorous with respect to the constraints within which the research has to be conducted. Research designed to inform policy often has to be undertaken under tighter constraints, and is often less rigorous, than that intended to satisfy the academic world. The policy maker is usually prepared to sacrifice some accuracy in the interests of obtaining usable information within a limited time-scale. However, if the constraints are too severe for the research to be conducted with reasonable rigour, then it is questionable whether the study is worth doing.

A characteristic of the human sciences that distinguishes from the physical sciences is their comparative looseness in the formulation of theory. This looseness is inevitable, deriving from the thought and behaviour of people which introduces a second level of variability in the research process. Predictions in the human sciences are at the mercy of many more uncontrolled variables than are predictions in the physical sciences. There have long been critiques of that false objectivity which ignores the role of what Dewey (1916: 326–7) called 'personal habits and interests'.[67]

The inherent unpredictability of people is captured by T.S. Eliot through the voice of Colby Simpkins in '*The confidential clerk*':

> I meant, there's no end to understanding a person
> All one can do is understand them better,
> To keep up with them; so that as the other changes
> You can understand the change as soon as it happens
> Though you couldn't have predicted it.
>
> (Eliot 1962: 247)

The desire for understanding the reasons for the behaviour of individuals points the researcher towards hermeneutic approaches to research consistent with the philosophical positions taken by writers such as Gadamer (1975) and Ricoeur (1981). However, some kinds of understanding are better gained from the broader perspective that large-scale, but more impersonal, research allows. Analogously, one can study coastal hydraulics by making observations at the water's edge, but one needs remote sensing from altitude to see the burgeoning of an *El Niño* oceanic current. We develop our broader understandings by patching together fragments of understanding that have been gained from different sources and different kinds of investigation. From time to time, weaknesses are revealed in some fragments, and they have to be discarded and be replaced by others. Researchers alternate between placing their weight on the leg of theory and on that of methodology – an ungainly way of describing walking, but one that perhaps captures the saccadic nature of progress.

The following chapter, by Braxton and Hirschy, shows how the former has, in collaboration with various colleagues, sought to test Tinto's theoretical propositions in order to establish where they hold up well, and where they do not. It illustrates the interplay between theory and methodology that is necessary if understanding is to be advanced.

7

Reconceptualizing antecedents of social integration in student departure

John M. Braxton and Amy S. Hirschy

Introduction

The puzzle of college student departure in the United States challenges scholars and practitioners. Tinto (1993) estimates that nearly one out of every two students in a two-year college and almost three out of ten students in four-year colleges and universities depart during their first year of college. Moreover, degree non-completion rates hover around 50 per cent for four-year colleges and universities and 56 per cent for two-year colleges (Tinto 1993). OECD statistics show that the 'survival rate' of French students is comparable, and that of Italian students markedly inferior, to that of the United States (Table 5.1). Consequently, college student departure also poses a problem in these countries. Such rates of departure and degree non-completion negatively affect the stability of institutional enrolments, budgets and the public perception of the quality of colleges and universities.

The 'departure puzzle' interests scholars and practitioners for different reasons. Practitioners express an interest in solving this puzzle in order to manage the enrolments of their colleges and universities. This puzzle intrigues scholars because not only is it a problem worthy of attention in its own right, but because departure also offers a window on the nature of the college student experience (Braxton et al. 1997).

The 'departure puzzle' has been the object of empirical attention in the United States for over 70 years. During the past 25 years, considerable progress on understanding this puzzle has occurred (Braxton 2000a). Although economic, organizational, psychological and sociological perspectives undergird studies of student departure (Tinto 1986), Tinto's Interactionalist Theory of college student departure holds paradigmatic status, as reflected in the number of citations received by his theoretical works (Tinto 1975, 1993). Using Web of Science data available from the Institute for Scientific Information (2002), we counted well over 700 citations.

Tinto's Interactionalist Theory

Tinto's Interactionalist Theory regards student departure as a result of the individual student's interaction with the college or university as an organization. The meanings the individual student ascribes to such interactions with the formal and informal dimensions of the college or university play a consequential role in student departure decisions (Tinto 1986, 1993; Braxton et al. 1997).

Tinto views the process of student retention as longitudinal (see Figure 7.1). Tinto (1975) states that students enter college with various individual characteristics (for example, family background, individual attributes and pre-college schooling experiences). These individual entry characteristics directly influence student departure decisions, as well as students' initial commitments to the institution (IC-1) and to the goal of college graduation (GC-1). Initial commitment to the institution and initial commitment to the goal of graduation, in turn, affect the level of a student's integration into the academic and social systems of the college or university.

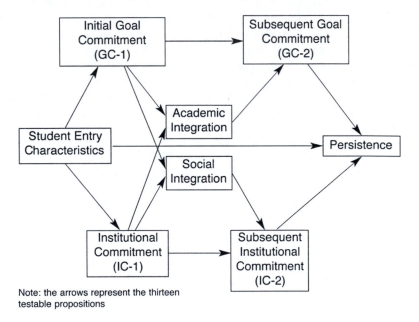

Figure 7.1 Path diagram of Tinto's Interactionalist Model of Student Persistence. (Source: Adapted from Tinto 1975)

Academic integration has structural and normative dimensions. Structural integration entails the meeting of explicit standards of the college or university, whereas normative integration pertains to an individual's identification with the normative structure of the academic system (Tinto 1975: 104).

Social integration refers to the extent of congruency between the individual student and the social system of a college or university.

Academic and social integration impact on the subsequent commitments of students. Specifically, the greater the student's level of academic integration, the greater the level of subsequent commitment to the goal of college graduation (GC-2). In addition, the greater the student's level of social integration, the greater the level of subsequent commitment to the focal college or university (IC-2) (Tinto 1975: 110). The student's initial levels of commitments – to institutional and graduation goals – also influence their level of subsequent commitments. In turn, the greater the levels of both subsequent institutional commitment and commitment to the goal of college graduation, the greater the likelihood the individual will persist in college.

Tinto's theory possesses logical internal consistency as the 13 testable propositions it yields are logically interconnected with one another (Braxton et al. 1997). Despite such logical internal consistency, an assessment of the empirical validity of this theory indicates that 5 of the 13 propositions receive strong backing from empirical tests of these propositions (Braxton et al. 1997).

Strong backing indicates that more than two-thirds of the empirical tests of these propositions produce confirming results. Consequently, these five propositions constitute reliable knowledge about the process of college student departure (Braxton 2000a). The five propositions have been isolated and are shown in Figure 7.2.

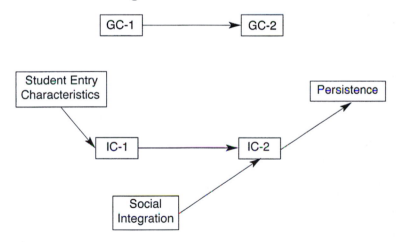

Note: the arrows indicate strongly-supported propositions

Figure 7.2 Path diagram of five strongly-supported propositions of Tinto's Interactionalist Model.

However, four of these propositions are logically interconnected. These four propositions take the following narrative form. Students enter college with various characteristics that influence their initial level of commitment to the college or university that they chose to attend. This initial level of institutional commitment also affects their subsequent commitment to the institution. Social integration also affects subsequent institutional commitment. The greater a student's degree of social integration, the greater the student's subsequent commitment to the institution. The greater the degree of a student's subsequent commitment to the institution, the greater the student's likelihood of persisting in college.

Delineating constructs through inductive processes

Although reliable knowledge about student departure obtains from these four robustly supported propositions, Tinto's theory requires serious revision (Braxton et al. 1997; Braxton 2000a). One approach to revision employs the above four propositions, but also focuses attention on the identification of factors that influence student integration into the social communities of colleges and universities (Braxton et al. 1997; Braxton 2000a).[68]

Braxton (2000a) recommends an inductive approach to the revision of Tinto's theory. Inductive theory construction entails the generation of underlying patterns of generalizations and understandings from empirical research on a focal phenomena (Wallace 1971). The concepts, generalizations, and understanding generated from this process provide the foundation for the development of a testable formal theory. Braxton (2000a) asserts that this inductive process also applies to the revision of an extant theory.

In this chapter, we apply the process of inductive theory construction to empirical tests focusing on factors that influence social integration, and review the findings of 62 tests that identify factors that impact on social integration in a statistically significant manner. These tests were conducted using traditionally-aged students in residential and commuter institutions. To identify a limited number of constructs that underlie the findings of these 62 tests, we engaged in a 'conceptual factor analysis' of these findings (Braxton 2000a). By identifying underlying concepts of the 62 tests, we conducted grounded theory revision. This inductive reasoning process is analogous to the open coding process in qualitative research (Strauss and Corbin 1998). Essentially, we carefully examined empirical findings to construct a parsimonious set of generalizations that influence social integration. Through this review, we identified three empirical generalizations (Wallace 1971) that undergird the significant influences on social integration. These constructs are the *commitment of the institution to student welfare, institutional integrity* and *communal potential.* In the following sections, we elaborate on each construct, present the findings that led to their generation, and offer propositions to modify Tinto's theory.

Commitment of the institution to student welfare

Commitment of the institution to student welfare manifests itself in an institution's abiding concern for the growth and development of its students. Student success – academically and socially – serves as an organizing principle for institutional action by faculty, administrators and staff. Faculty members make professional choices designed to enhance student academic and intellectual development by conducting their courses to facilitate student learning. Through more informal means, faculty also interact with students outside the classroom. Administrators and staff display a desire to assist students in their adjustment to college via programmes, policies and personal contact. Love (1995) emphasizes the importance of considering the roles non-faculty professionals play with respect to student outcomes, including retention. In short, faculty, staff and administrators care about student learning and adjustment to the campus community.

An institution committed to the welfare of its students clearly communicates that it greatly values students in groups as well as individuals. Respect for students as individuals and the equal treatment of students constitute further manifestations of such an institutional commitment. Students attending an institution that exhibits such a commitment perceive that they, like administrators, faculty and staff, also have a stake in membership in the communities of the institution.

This construct resonates with two of Tinto's (1993) three principles of effective retention – a steadfast commitment of the institution to the students it serves and a commitment of the institution to the education of all of its students.

The construct springs from several different patterns of research findings. Such aspects of the commitment of the institution to the welfare of the student as the valuing of students, respect for students as individuals, the equal treatment of students, and assuring students that they have a stake in the communities of the college or university stem from the effects of three forms of organizational behaviour on the integration of students into collegiate social communities. Specifically, fairness in the administration of policies and rules (Berger and Braxton 1998), communication of institutional policies and requirements (Berger and Braxton 1998; Braxton and Brier 1998), and giving students a say in decision-making about institutional policies and rules (Berger and Braxton 1998) positively affect student social integration.

The equal treatment of students and respect for students as individuals also stem from the effects of perceived campus racial discrimination on social integration. More specifically, the greater the level of perceived campus racial discrimination, the lower the level of social integration for African-American students (Cabrera et al. 1999), Latino students (Hurtado and Carter 1997) and non-minority students (Nora and Cabrera 1996).

Concern for student success and adjustment to college emanates from findings regarding orientation programme attendance. Nora et al. (1990) found that such 'getting ready' behaviours as early expectations for college and pre-matriculation experiences with the college facilitate the social integration of community college students. Also, attending a two-day orientation programme for first-year students impacts in a positive way the social integration of students in a residential university (Pascarella et al. 1986).

Concern for student learning, a critical aspect of an institution's commitment to the welfare of students, stems from the positive influences of faculty use of active learning practices (Braxton, Milem et al. 2000) and the faculty teaching skills of organization and preparation and instructional clarity (Braxton, Bray et al. 2000) on student social integration. Active learning (Johnson et al. 1991; Anderson and Adams 1992) and faculty teaching skills of organization and preparation and instructional clarity also yield positive impacts on college student learning (Cohen 1989; Pascarella et al. 1996; Feldman 1998). Yorke (1999b) found that a poor quality of the student experience, as defined by the quality of teaching, the level of support offered by staff, and how the academic programme is organized, was implicated in student attrition.

Institutional integrity

Colleges and universities true to their espoused mission and goals best depict the construct of institutional integrity. A college or university exhibits institutional integrity if the actions of its administrators, faculty and staff are congruent with the mission and goals it promulgates. Institutional integrity may also manifest itself in the various public and institutional documents disseminated by the institution to both its constituents and the lay public. Institutional integrity also entails institutional action that is congruent with such academic values as academic freedom and the principle of merit.

The construct of institutional integrity springs from two configurations of findings. First, fairness in the administration of institutional policies and rules positively affects student social integration (Berger and Braxton 1998). This finding exemplifies institutional integrity, as the principle of merit finds expression in fairness in the administration of policies and rules. At base, the principle of merit requires equal treatment of individuals rather than treatment based on social or personal characteristics. Second, students' unmet expectations for college may stem from a lack of institutional integrity between admissions publications and information and life at the focal college or university. Specifically, the more a student perceives that their social expectations for college are being met, the greater their degree of social integration (Helland et al. 2001–2002). The fulfilment of expectations for academic and intellectual development and the fulfilment of expectations for career development also affect social integration in a positive manner (Braxton et al. 1995).

Communal potential

Communal potential refers to the degree to which a student perceives that a subgroup of students exists within the college community with which that student could share similar values, beliefs and goals. Astin (1984) offers a useful definition of community, defining it as small subgroup of students espousing a common purpose through which group identity, a sense of cohesion and uniqueness develops.

Communities emerge from residence halls (Berger 1997), the classroom (Tinto 1997, 2000) and student peer groups (Newcomb 1966).

Communal potential looms as particularly important for students whose cultures of origin are different from the predominant culture of a given college or university. Kuh and Love (2000) present a pertinent proposition: 'the probability of persistence is inversely related to the cultural distance between a student's culture(s) or origin and the cultures of immersion'. For such students, attaining a sense of membership in one or more cultural enclaves is critical. A cultural enclave is a group or subgroup holding values, attitudes and beliefs similar to a student's culture of origin (Kuh and Love 2000).

Several configurations of findings give rise to the construct of communal potential. First, a sense of community in the residence hall fosters social integration (Berger 1997). Specifically, Berger (1997) identified three elements of community in residence halls as exerting a positive influence on student social integration: identity, solidarity and interaction. Identity is the extent to which students value the community in their residence halls (McMillan and Chavis 1986). Solidarity pertains to the degree to which students in a residence hall hold similar views, beliefs and goals and a desire to work together when problems arise (McMillan and Chavis 1986). Community interaction is the frequency and intensity of interactions among students living in a residence hall.

Second, the social approach and social avoidance behaviours students use to cope with stress influence a student's sense of community. To elaborate, formal and informal social approach behaviours positively affect social integration, whereas social avoidance behaviours wield a negative influence (Eaton and Bean 1995). Informal social approach behaviours relate to social choices made by students and their social interactions (for example, attending informal parties with friends). Formal social approach behaviours pertain to a student's level of participation in campus leadership and the

formal social structure (for example, holding office in a campus organization). Social avoidance behaviours are actions that take a student away from
campus, such as going home for the weekend (Eaton and Bean 1995).

  Third, student peer groups also foster social integration. More specifically, the social support students receive from their college peers exerts a
positive influence on their degree of social integration (Milem and Berger
1997; Berger and Milem 1999). Moreover, an aspect of the social networks
embedded in student sub-groups also fosters social integration: the greater
the extent to which a student is named by other students as someone with
whom they frequently talk, the greater the student's degree of social integration (Thomas 2000).

Toward a revision of Tinto's theory

The constructs of *commitment of the institution to student welfare, institutional
integrity* and *communal potential* provide a basis for the revision of Tinto's
Interactionist Theory. The revision of Tinto's theory presented here
includes the four interconnected propositions of Tinto's theory that receive
strong empirical support. However, this revision centres on *commitment of the
institution to student welfare, institutional integrity* and *communal potential* as
important antecedents of social integration (Figure 7.3).

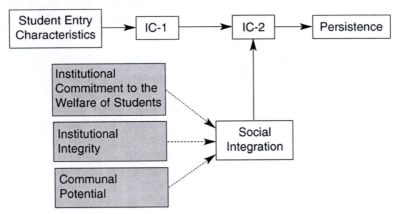

Note: shaded boxes indicate new constructs; dotted-lined arrows indicate new propositions

Figure 7.3   Path diagram of conceptual model with commitment to the welfare of
   the student, institutional integrity and communal potential as antecedents to
   social integration, subsequent institutional commitment and subsequent persistence.

In the following section, we present a revision of Tinto's theory in narrative
form. First, we discuss how commitment of the institution to student welfare, institutional integrity and communal potential relate to social

integration. Next, we identify recommendations for further inquiries and empirical testing of our hypotheses in future studies.

Antecedents to social integration

Braxton (2000a) asserts that scholars must make careful distinctions among antecedents of social integration, social integration and the outcomes of social integration. He posits that social integration emerges from a student's experiences with the social communities of a college or university. Students experience social integration if they feel a sense of normative congruence and social affiliation with members of the social communities of a college or university (Durkheim 1951; Tinto 1975). As a consequence, antecedents of social integration are those forces that shape a student's perception of their extent of social integration. Accordingly, student perceptions of *commitment of the institution to student welfare, institutional integrity* and *communal potential* emerge from the interpretations they make from their experiences with administrators, faculty, staff and student peers.

The social context of the institution

Tinto's Interactionalist Theory centres upon the contacts between students and a single college or university and how students' interpretations of those interactions affect their decisions to persist at the institution. It follows that individual students and the institution hold distinguishing characteristics that affect day-to-day interactions. Put differently, just as students possess unique life experiences, (for example, student entry characteristics, goals, expectations), each institution exists in a particular context. Individual colleges and universities possess distinct histories, missions, values and traditions held by their own academic communities. These values and traditions reflect an organizational culture which guides the behaviour of individuals and groups affiliated with the institution (Kuh and Whitt 1988). The culture can be discerned by the manner in which the members of the campus community (faculty, students, staff and administrators) interact with each other and how the common values are communicated through tradition, policy and practice. Over time, the daily interactions provide a means by which students can detect and evaluate how their values compare with the larger community (Tinto 1993). In other words, the manner in which campus community members express the organizational culture of the institution affects students' perceptions of the social context of the institution. Further, these perceptions of the institution influence the degree to which students integrate into the community, because social integration refers to the extent of congruency between the individual student and the social system of a college or university.

One must consider the conditions in society which provide the context for individual integration (Durkheim 1951; Tinto 1993). In the case of colleges and universities, the three constructs defined earlier – *commitment of the institution to student welfare, institutional integrity* and *communal potential* – offer ways to understand organizational conditions that provide the context for social integration into the college or university community.

Commitment of the institution to student welfare: a theoretical proposition

Interactions with faculty, staff and administrators influence a student's perception of the institution's commitment to the welfare of students. Given the intellectual and social challenges inherent in the college experience, as well as those in navigating the numerous administrative tasks necessary to make educational progress (for example, course selection and registration, financial aid applications, etc.), the student experience engenders difficulties. Stress can serve a useful, motivating purpose, yet a balance is necessary for optimal performance (Whitman et al. 1984). Students need to experience a balance of challenge and support for personal growth and development (Sanford 1966), and faculty, staff and administrators who are committed to student welfare can ameliorate the stress students feel by how they interact with students. Those committed to the welfare of students strive to treat students fairly, inclusively, and with respect. The manner in which they interact with students (both directly through personal contact and indirectly through making decisions that affect students) indicates that they value students as community members, and they are concerned about student growth and development in and out of the classroom.

The degree to which a person perceives that he or she is noticed, recognized, and/or valued by others also matters (Rosenberg and McCullough 1981), and is influenced by the educational setting (Schlossberg et al. 1989). As such, students who perceive that they matter to faculty, staff and administrators may be more likely to want to be connected to those individuals. Further, when students sense that others want them to succeed, they may devote more psychological energy toward the tasks of integrating into the community (Astin 1984).

Other indicators of a commitment to the welfare of students include clear, fair institutional policies and procedures that are communicated to students. When possible, students are consulted (individually or in representative groups) and otherwise involved in decisions that affect them. Involving students in influencing campus policies demonstrates that they share a stake in the community. If students feel they can make a difference, they are more likely to take an active approach to learning and social situations, and they are more likely to invest energy into their educational and social experience at the institution. Students who take active approaches in college are better integrated academically and socially (Astin 1984; Eaton and Bean 1995).

In contrast, unclear, conflicting policies; unhelpful bureaucratic responses; passive classroom learning environments; and unfriendly, combative encounters with administrators, faculty or staff may be indicators that some community members do not highly value the welfare of students. Students who perceive such disdain may be less likely to feel comfortable seeking out additional interactions with the college or university personnel. Some students avoid situations in an effort to reduce stress (Eaton and Bean 1995). Worse still, students who need help and do not ask for it risk further isolation, resulting in malintegration. Poor integration results when students are insufficiently affiliated with members of the college community (Tinto 1993).

Students who perceive a strong institutional commitment to the welfare of students will be more likely to want and be able to participate in the formal and informal realms of the collegiate environment. Students who perceive that others are willing to assist them may be more likely to ask for help when they need it, and those who perceive a supportive environment will be more likely to make connections with others in the community. Therefore, a high level of institutional commitment to the welfare of the student facilitates social integration. The formulations above lead to the following proposition: *the greater the level of institutional commitment to the welfare of the student, the more likely it is that the student will achieve social integration.*

Institutional integrity: a theoretical proposition

A college or university exhibits institutional integrity if the actions of its administrators, faculty and staff are congruent with the mission and goals promulgated by the institution.

Through day-to-day interactions, student perceptions form around the consistency of institutional actions with the college or university's stated missions and goals. If interactions with administrators, faculty or staff are discordant with the shared purposes and values of the institution, the student may feel confused, disappointed, even betrayed. Conflicts between institutional goals and how they are implemented send incongruous messages and undermine the student's understanding of the institution. Such interactions belie a level of trust that students may have in the institution. When that trust is damaged, the student may feel distanced from the community and become less inclined to participate. Additionally, students may generalize negative experiences with an individual or office to other faculty, staff and/or administrators, which can lead to decreased interactions with college or university personnel. These kinds of experiences result in increased isolation, which hinders social integration.

As an example, colleges and universities devote significant financial resources to communicate the mission and goals of the institution to prospective students and their families through the admissions process. Hence, upon arrival, students have expectations regarding many areas of the college experience. If a student's interpretation of the stated institutional goals is congruent with their perception of subsequent actions by administrators, faculty and staff, then the student may derive confidence from anticipating what to expect from the institution. A higher level of confidence may positively influence a student's desire to make connections with others within the community. Perceiving interactions that coincide with stated goals indicates a degree of stability that students in the flux of transition may especially value. Hence, if a student's expectations shaped by the institution's stated missions and goals are met through day-to-day interactions with college or university personnel, then the student is more likely to achieve social integration. Therefore, a high level of institutional integrity facilitates social integration. The formulations above lead to the following proposition: *the greater the level of institutional integrity, the more likely it is that the student will achieve social integration.*

Communal potential: a theoretical proposition

Whereas the previous two constructs involve how students perceive faculty, staff and administrative actions, the communal potential construct focuses on student perceptions of the relationships and values shared among their peers. In short, this construct pertains to the degree to which a student perceives that there is the possibility of an affinity group for them to join in the student community.

Distinguishing between the constructs 'communal potential' and 'social integration' may be helpful. First, there is a temporal difference between communal potential and social integration. An antecedent to social integration, communal potential involves perceptions by students that pertain to the capacity of the social environment, not the relationships a student has already formed. These perceptions are shaped by interactions among students. Second, where perceptions of the communal potential involve only peers, social integration includes the broader college community (that is, students, faculty, staff and administrators). The communal potential construct refers to the perception that there is a possible group of students with which a student would like to connect. Social integration refers to the extent of congruence between the individual student and the social system of the institution and the affiliations a student actually holds within the institutional community.

The communal potential construct refers to a student's perception of the likelihood of meaningful social relationships in the student community.

Kuh (2001–2002) advocates the consideration of subgroups of students versus the larger institutional enrolment when studying influences on persistence, particularly in large institutions, where a 'coherent, salient, campus culture' rarely exists (Kuh 2001–2002: 25). Even if a dominant student culture prevails, a student may perceive that the values of the student community as a whole are different from their own, yet interacts with a smaller group of students with whom they share similar values. Such subcommunities can be located in various places: in classrooms, on residence hall floors, in student clubs and organizations, through theatre productions, and on the intramural field. In this case, the student's connection with the affinity group or cultural enclave (Kuh and Love 2000) can facilitate social integration. In other words, the congruence that facilitates social integration would be between the student and the smaller group of students, not the larger student community as a whole.

It is not the scope of the larger student community culture that matters as an antecedent to social integration as much as the qualities that students perceive among the student body that offer potential for social connection. Students who perceive multiple opportunities to connect with classmates who share their values, beliefs and attitudes are more likely to make contact with those individuals. Interacting more frequently with peers in the community leads to greater social integration. Therefore, a high level of communal potential facilitates social integration. The formulations above lead to the following proposition: *the stronger the student's perception of the communal potential on campus, the more likely it is that the student will achieve higher levels of social integration.*

Future research

Though Tinto's Interactionalist Theory is considered paradigmatic, researchers continually refine, refute and extend the theory of student departure. By using inductive theory construction, a review of empirical findings of factors that influence social integration resulted in the following propositions:

1. The greater level of institutional commitment to the welfare of the student, the more likely the student will achieve social integration. The greater level of social integration, the more likely the student will achieve subsequent institutional commitment and persist in higher education.
2. The greater level of institutional integrity, the more likely the student will achieve social integration. The greater level of social integration, the more likely the student will achieve subsequent institutional commitment and persist in higher education.
3. The stronger the student's perception of the communal potential on campus, the more likely the student will achieve higher levels of social integration. The greater the level of social integration, the more likely

the student will achieve subsequent institutional commitment and persist in higher education.

In each case since social integration has been found to have strong links to subsequent institutional commitment and indirectly to persistence, additional inquiry is required. Scholars are invited to develop and test these three propositions and their influence on social integration. Other antecedents to social integration should be identified and tested as well. Ascertaining which factors lead to commitment of the institution to the welfare of students, institutional integrity and communal potential is another possible venue for future research.

Examining the propositions in various institutional types (for example, commuter, residential, two-year, four-year, colleges and universities) will illuminate the effectiveness of the constructs in different contexts. In the case of commuter institutions in which student populations tend to be older with more part-time enrollees, for example, the influence of social integration on subsequent institutional commitment is not a strongly supported proposition (Braxton et al. 1997). Perhaps the constructs explored in this paper influence subsequent institutional commitment directly, and indirectly affect persistence in commuter and other institutional settings.

Finally, these new constructs can also be useful in studying student departure decisions in contexts beyond the United States. Understanding more about what colleges and universities can do to facilitate social integration and subsequent institutional commitment could have important effects on student persistence rates around the globe.

8

Why students leave their programmes

Qualitative contributions to understanding

In Chapter 6 we noted the theoretical complexity inherent in the literature on retention – a complexity that is greater than current formulations allow. Some of that complexity can be found in the studies typically conducted in US institutions where the numbers of students are sufficient for path-analytic methodology to be applied. These produce 'macro' depictions of student characteristics and behaviours, and are often used, inferentially, as indicative of behavioural propensities. What such studies lack is detail of the influences that bore on individual students' departure decisions. For that, the need is for studies with a qualitative component.[69] Without qualitative exemplifications, the abstractions of models lack 'life' and are difficult for those without a grounding in psychometrics (that is, most people dealing with the related issues of retention and student success) to interpret. The notion of student-faculty interaction, for example, is made very intelligible when a student says:

> I think that in sociology and humanities, the quality of the teachers was better. They were more interested in teaching you. They seemed more interested if you learned something, rather than the grade you got. The biology teachers were just interested in telling you what they had learned, and you'd better learn it too.
>
> White male who switched from science
> (Seymour and Hewitt 1997: 148)

This chapter focuses primarily on findings from two fairly large-scale surveys of full-time and sandwich[70] students who withdrew from their programmes in institutions in the UK. These surveys both involved a number of institutions of varying types and offer reference points ('benchmarks' would be too strong a word) for the outcomes of the surveys that are now conducted in many individual institutions. Each obtained qualitative data in order to illuminate its statistical aspect.

Why students leave their programmes

The reasons why students leave their programmes can be grouped into four general categories:

- Flawed decision-making about entering the programme;
- Students' experience of the programme and the institution generally;
- Failure to cope with the demand of the programme; and
- Events that impact on students' lives outside the institution.

The boundaries between the categories are not clear-cut, particularly that between the second and third. Institutions can influence the second considerably, and can contribute in varying extents to the first and third. The fourth, self-evidently, lies almost entirely beyond institutional influence. In general, students on part-time programmes show a greater propensity than their full-time peers to be affected by extra-institutional matters, and lesser propensities to make poor decisions regarding entry and to reject the experience of higher education. In this chapter, the emphasis is on factors that influence student departure, and it must be borne in mind that the evidence that is presented comes from students who withdrew from their programmes. Chapters 9 and 10 address the issues that are raised here.

The publication of the first set of institutional performance data (HEFCE 1999b), coupled with high-profile comment in the media, has probably been the greatest stimulus to institutions in the UK to research the retention and completion of their students. Institutions had previously undertaken investigations into retention since the establishment of working parties on performance indicators in the 1990s had signalled that this was an emergent political issue. Nowadays it is commonplace for institutions to make substantial use of their student records systems for research into retention and completion, and to follow up students who have withdrawn in order to establish their reason(s) for having done so.

Whilst there has been considerable work on retention in individual institutions in the UK,[71] very little has entered the public domain – in notable contrast to the position in the US, where intra-institutional retention analyses are regularly presented at the forums run by the Association for Institutional Research (AIR).

In UK higher education there have been two fairly large quantitative 'autopsy' studies seeking to understand the reasons for students' withdrawal from higher education, by Yorke (1999b)[72] and by Davies and Elias (2003). Asking withdrawn students why they left their programmes risks various kinds of bias, including non-response, self-justification, misattribution of cause, selective memory, distortion due to the passage of time, and so on. Yet any attempt to understand, longitudinally, how influences build up to a student's decision to withdraw also presents formidable methodological difficulties.[73] Both Yorke and Davies and Elias sought, in their different ways, to get students to comment on their withdrawals in an attempt to gain a fuller understanding than mere 'ticking of response boxes' would allow. Both studies received from some students extended comments which, on the face of it, seem plausible – not only in respect of what was said, but also the manner in which it was said. For example, one mature student in Yorke's work, who had to make arrangements for childcare, wrote:

> As a mature, married student with a minimum of 2 hours travelling time there and back, I found [university's] course too inflexible to accommodate my individual needs. Travelling for a total of 4 hours to attend a 1 hour lecture or tutorial only, was not sensible or constructive, yet I was told I *must*. [...] Leaving house at 8am and returning at 7pm and still having work to do, meant that relationships with friends, family and husband deteriorated to the point of being nonexistent. I approached the mature-student counsellor who said that no concession could be made. NOT HELPFUL!
>
> Student reading Law. (Yorke 1999a: 29 (emphasis in the original))

Not every student comment was as dramatically expressed as that, of course, but there were very few instances where the criterion of plausibility might not have been met. In circumstances such as these, the researcher has to weigh up the evidence and draw conclusions on the balance of probabilities rather than appeal to an unattainable higher standard of proof.

When the Labour government took office in the UK in 1997, it moved quickly to replace free tuition with a requirement for students to contribute towards tuition fees, and to replace the maintenance grant with a system of loans, the latter being introduced in two stages. Yorke's study surveyed students who had left their institutions[74] in the north-west of England between 1994 and 1996, and hence the government's changes had not taken place at the time of their decision to withdraw. Davies and Elias' survey of ex-students was broadly similar, but covered a national sample of 30 institutions and students who had withdrawn during the academic years 1996–97 and 1998–99. This study, therefore, involved students who had enrolled in higher education on both sides of the implementation of the Labour government's policy on student funding.

The study reported by Yorke obtained responses from 2151 full-time and sandwich students (response rate 32 per cent); that by Davies and Elias attracted 1510 responses (response rate 10 per cent). It should be noted that the latter study covered a wide range of topics, which is likely to have been a disincentive to the completion of the questionnaire by students.

General influences on student withdrawal, as found in these two studies, are shown in Table 8.1. The picture painted by the two studies is broadly similar despite the changes in funding for students. Davies and Elias did not ask their respondents about the quality of the student experience, so no significance can be attached to its absence from the right-hand column.

The profile of influences, as found in these two studies, varied with the age of the student. Yorke found that the older entrants were about half as likely as their younger peers to make the wrong choice of field of study,

Table 8.1   Influences on full-time and sandwich students' early departure from their programmes.

Yorke (1999b)	Davies and Elias (2003)
Wrong choice of field of study	Wrong choice of course
Academic difficulties	Financial problems
Financial problems	Personal problems
Poor quality of the student experience	Academic difficulties
Unhappiness with the social environment	Wrong choice of institution
Dissatisfaction with institutional provision	

and were less likely to be dissatisfied with accommodation. These differences are possibly attributable to (a) greater maturity, with older students having a clearer view of what they wanted to achieve in higher education; and (b) older students being to a greater extent rooted in communities and hence exhibiting less transience in their accommodation. These older students were more likely to experience financial difficulty, to suffer from the demands of employment whilst studying, and to be responsible for dependants (it may be plausible to infer that, for some students, these are connected). Davies and Elias' data for full-time and sandwich students are consistent with Yorke's in indicating that the wrong choice of course is a much less potent influence for older students, as is dissatisfaction with accommodation. Davies and Elias found that, for older students, financial difficulty was most frequently cited, followed by the rather amorphous 'personal problems', and difficulties with academic study.

Flawed decision-making

Of Yorke's respondents, 39 per cent indicated that they had chosen the wrong field of study, and there was a close association with the recognition that the programme was not relevant to the student's intended career (23 per cent, though it is unclear whether the career had been identified at the time of enrolment) and – perhaps consequentially – a lack of commitment to the programme (38 per cent). This cluster of influences was noticeably more prominent for young entrants than for their older counterparts. Davies and Elias (2003) found that mistaken choice of course was influential in the withdrawal of 21.1 per cent of their male respondents, and in that of 25.5 per cent of their female respondents. The researchers observed that additional advice would probably not have influenced the deliberate choices that some students made – these students only realized they had made a mistake once they had embarked on their chosen programme (Davies and Elias 2003: 30). One might hope that all students would make good choices, but the sheer complexity of the decision-making process (in which academic and personal goals have to be melded) means that this is unrealistic in practice. However, Davies and Elias (2003: 36) did find, in telephone conversations with some of their students, that students were much more thorough in selecting a programme the second time around, not least because they had better appreciated what they really wanted to do and the questions they needed to ask in order to ensure that there was an acceptable match between this and the programme they were considering.

It is possible that the requirement to pay tuition fees 'up front' since 1997 may have sharpened the focus of intending students on the choice of a study programme, and that this accounts for the lower incidence of unsatisfactory choice of programme. However, other factors may have played a part – notably the publicity given to retention and completion since the publication of the first set of performance data for UK institutions (HEFCE 1999a).

What might lead to flawed decision-making? Students' uncertainty regarding what they want to do; family and/or school pressure; a lack of appreciation of what their chosen programme involves; poor careers advice at school; and the inadequate provision of information by institutions may contribute, individually or in combination.

Some students responding to one or other of the surveys mentioned that their primary motivation was social in some respect – to get away from home, to go to a particular city, or to join up with friends or family at a particular institution. The lack of educational focus is exemplified by 'CL', who seemed more concerned to escape his home environment than to embark on a programme:

> I just wanted a route out of my home town: I didn't research the courses available to me. I never appreciated how important it was to work at getting it right.
>
> (Davies and Elias 2003: 32)

'Irene', in a qualitative study of student departure undertaken in one institution, clearly made her decision to enrol too hastily:

> ... I wasn't having a particularly happy time personally and I just thought I'll do what the school says, and once I actually got to it [the institution] I realised that maybe it wasn't the only option and maybe I could be happier doing something else...
>
> (Longden 2001b: 30)

The 'natural' expectation of entry to university distracted another student from the need for clarity in deciding what to do:

> Definitely went to university because I had always assumed the route school-uni-job and although I wasn't pressured, it was expected by school, friends, family, even myself.
>
> Student reading Mathematics (Yorke 1999b: 43)

The danger of drifting on into higher education was exemplified by 'HD':

> My A-levels were geared towards accounts and economics, and I just carried on in that direction and didn't think of anything else. I should have researched it all a bit more.
>
> (Davies and Elias 2003: 32)

For another student, the choice of programme was strongly influenced by a combination of parental pressure and perhaps dubious advice:

> I had no idea what I wanted to do after my A levels and was advised to do Sociology as it was a general subject that could lead to many professions. Not only did I dislike the course, I was pushed into Uni by my parents...
>
> Student reading Social Sciences (Yorke 1999b: 43)

A number of respondents to Davies and Elias' survey were very critical of the advice that they had received whilst attending school. 'AM' commented:

> It was the worst advice I have ever had. I had wanted to do graphic design when I was at school, and they said that it was a cut-throat business and that I would not be able to hold down a job ... They put me onto engineering: they hadn't a clue about me.
>
> (Davies and Elias 2003: 30)

Too little, too late, seems to have been the experience of 'AF' when being advised regarding her application for a place:

> We only had one meeting with them and that was at the time we were filling in our UCAS forms. So, they were really just vetting the choices we had already made, not helping us to make those choices. We could go and see them whenever we wanted to, but only one meeting was compulsory. I think we could have done with more.
>
> (Davies and Elias 2003: 30)

However, it needs to be noted that AF made no use of the opportunity for meetings initiated by herself.

Choosing a hobby as the subject of degree study may not necessarily be a good move. One student realized, too late in the day, that she should have kept her hobby and her studies in separate life-compartments:

> I had always enjoyed [performance art] but realised ... that it was very intense and that I enjoyed it purely as a hobby and did not want to make a career of it. [...] My career objectives had always swung between Nursing and [performance art]. It was only after I commenced the course that I realised that I was not committed enough to [performance art] and that I wanted to do Nursing.
>
> Student reading Performance Arts (Yorke 1999a: 11)

Some students clearly had not appreciated what their chosen programme of study entailed. This could be due to inadequate information from the institution (the occasional student went so far as to allege misinformation) and/or a failure on the part of the student to find out what was likely to face them. One student on a medicine-related programme claimed to have received 'no information that we would be studying dead bodies', an activity that she had found disturbing. Others realized too late that they were ill-equipped for the programme that they had chosen:

> [My] Mathematics not up to the standard required. It was very difficult and the course content was not explained before I embarked on it.
> Student reading Engineering (Yorke 1999b: 43)

Another was faced with being in a class containing students learning a language *ab initio* and those who already held an A Level pass in the language:

> The course was not designed for people with no knowledge of Spanish. After the first semester of year 1, we were expected to have A level standard and knowledge of Spanish – impossible! Teachers expected us to learn vocab from reading newspapers and dictionaries – if we didn't or couldn't pick up the vocab then we were blamed for not trying enough.
> Student reading Joint Honours including Spanish (Yorke 1999a: 10)

Some students find their programmes insufficiently challenging, whereas others are overstretched. 'Frances' (whose sense of disappointment began in the social environment of the student union) and 'Eve' illustrate the contrast:

> To be honest it was like being back in primary school again. [...] I was so frustrated, having been to grammar school I was used to there being a certain standard of education, there were no thick people at my school and to be honest it was really frustrating to be in a lecture understanding what they were saying and waiting to get on with it and the person next to you is saying I don't understand explain it to me.
> 'Frances' (Longden 2001b: 47–8)

> I knew there'd be a lot of work involved but I didn't expect that much work. It was also of a much higher standard than I expected.
> 'Eve' (Longden 2001b: 32)

The provision of information is clearly an institutional responsibility – as the UK Advertising Standards Authority requires, it should be 'legal, decent, honest and truthful'. However, there is a limit to what an institution can provide in paper or electronic form, and open days and other opportunities to visit offer putative students the chance to gain a fuller understanding of the nature of the academic programme and support services that are available. Prospectuses are advertisements which seek to portray an institution in its best light – happy-looking students, students concentrating on their work, sunlit buildings, and not a hint of rain.[75] The social opportunities available in the hinterland are typically promoted, occasionally to excess.

Others, too, offer information to the intending student. Guides to choosing institutions are available in many countries, often backed up by so-called 'league tables' or 'rankings' based on the summation of scores on a range of variables such as entry scores; research performance; spending on resources; and so on. The institutional vignettes are too brief to be of practical use, and the tabulations have been widely criticized[76] on a variety of grounds – not least because they give the prospective student no indication of the kind of experience they can expect. Even when teaching quality assessments were incorporated, it was widely appreciated that a high rating did not necessarily mean that the student experience would correspond, since institutions had learned how to present themselves to best advantage. The Quality Assurance Agency (QAA) reports on institutional provision in broad subject areas[77] do, however, offer the diligent inquirer both a broad view of the strengths and weaknesses of an institution, and also implicitly provide some starting-points for discussion when a prospective student visits an institution.

We noted in Chapter 5 that surveys of graduate opinion might be less useful to potential applicants than they might assume. There is also a danger that students will rely too much on institutional reputation when making their choices. Whilst an award from an institution high in the reputational range is likely to be more of a 'positional good' than one from a lower position, the actual programme may not fit what the student wants. The following cautionary tale illustrates the point:

> The languages courses at [institution] had an extremely high literature/history bias and, personally, I wanted to find a course with more language teaching – less traditional. I found ... my pure language skills were deteriorating which depressed me and made me lose interest in the course itself. [...] I should have been better informed by my 6th Form about the differences between red-brick universities vs new universities. The snob value attached to red-brick universities is unfortunate because they are certainly not always the best choice.
>
> Student reading Languages (Yorke 1999a: 13)

A successful matching of student to programme and institution requires a number of factors to be taken into account, and for those involved (including careers advisers and family members) to have the underpinning knowledge necessary for the advice they give to be properly grounded. Rapid decision-making runs the risk of being superficial: the 'clearing' admissions process in the UK, which takes place in a short period in late summer following the publication of the A Level examination results, is not conducive to good decision-making. Davies and Elias (2003: 46) show that, for their sample of withdrawn students, the incidences of poor choice of programme and of institution were around one-third higher for 'clearing' students than for those who had entered higher education by the normal procedure operated by the Universities and Colleges Admissions Service (UCAS).

Some students are, at the age of 18, not yet ready for the demands of higher education. One third of a sample of young Australian students admitted as much in responding to surveys conducted by McInnis and James (1995) and McInnis et al. (2000).[78] At that age, students may not have developed a sufficiently strong sense of purpose to carry them through the ups and downs of being a student, in which case a period out of formal education might prove valuable – not only in helping them to determine what they really want to do, but also to build up some financial reserves to help them pay their way through degree study.

Many students take up accommodation that may or may not have been subject to a process of approval by the institution. Often this extra-institutional accommodation is at the cheap end of the market and in relatively rough neighbourhoods (the latter may not have been appreciated by the student arriving from a distance). The primary involvement of the institution is typically limited to providing lists of possible accommodations, and this might be extended to the provision of a commentary on the character of the areas concerned. Beyond that, it becomes a matter for the student to arrange the rental.

Institutions have greater responsibility where they own accommodation, in that they have to pay attention to matters such as security and to the behaviour of the students. A few students commented that they had found an institutional hall of residence constraining, either because of a lack of privacy or because the hall environment was not conducive to studying. There is something of a trend away from institutional ownership of residential accommodation, and for new purpose-built accommodation to be constructed and managed by private companies.

Quality of the student experience

Since Davies and Elias (2003) did not ask their sample of ex-students about the quality of their experiences in higher education, the only substantial dataset of such comments is that collected by Yorke and colleagues. At first glance, it is surprising that the focus groups involved in research for the National Audit Office (NAO 2002a) did not cite teaching quality as a main influence on withdrawal, but this may be due to 'teaching' being given a narrow interpretation. Feedback on work, for example, was given prominence in the NAO report (NAO 2002a: para. 2.21), and it can be argued persuasively that feedback is a vital component of teaching.

The most frequently cited influences on students' departure, as found by Yorke and colleagues, are given in Table 8.2.

The data in Table 8.2 derive from a factor analysis of the survey responses, and these items are the six that loaded most heavily on the 'Poor quality of the student experience' factor.[79] Also loading on that factor, but slightly less

Table 8.2   The influence of the quality of the student experience on withdrawal

Item	Percentage indicating moderate or considerable influence (N = 2151)
Teaching did not suit me	31
Programme organization	27
Inadequate staff support outside timetable	24
Lack of personal support from staff	24
Quality of teaching	23
Class sizes too large	16

Source: Yorke (1999b: 38)

heavily than on the 'Wrong choice of programme' factor was 'Programme not what I expected', which – as noted above – was influential on 37 per cent of the sample. For around a quarter of respondents, then, there was unhappiness with the teaching and personal support they received from staff, and with aspects of the way in which their programmes were organized. The impersonality implicit in their views about support are perhaps reflected to some extent in the belief that class sizes were too large.

Elaborative comment on teaching was sparse. Some respondents commented adversely on lecture delivery and on the lack of opportunity to take good notes for later use. Their difficulties may have stemmed from a change from the teaching methods to which they had become accustomed: in the case of Medicine, the shift to a problem-based approach may have been particularly challenging for students whose learning experiences had hitherto been more traditional in character. Some students disliked working in seminar groups and tutorials, one Social Science student noting that they were 'extremely intimidating and cold', and another observing that they tended to be dominated by the very self-confident.

Comment was sharper regarding the supportiveness of staff, mainly with reference to times outside the formal teaching schedule. A student who had entered from an access course found the level of personal support in her higher education institution to fall short of what she felt she needed:

> I completed an access course prior to attending [university] where the staff were really helpful and knew you on a 1 to 1 basis. At university this wasn't the case and ... I couldn't cope with the workload without no tutorial support.
> Student reading for a Diploma in Higher Education
> (Yorke 1999b: 40)

Another student who had entered Engineering with a BTEC (Business and Technology Education Council) qualification instead of A Level, found that his Mathematics was inadequate. The lack of support from staff had diminished his commitment and interest to such an extent that he left his programme.

The off-handedness of tutors in one student's Art and Design programme was picked up in the following comment:

> The course was taught very loosely, the tutors were never around to help, and when they were, they were very unhelpful. They were critical of your work to the point of being rude, not constructive criticism, if your work was not the best, average, then you were ignored in favour of the best students. ... the way one tutor spoke to me ... has put me off higher education and will take a long time considering ever going back.
>
>   Student reading Art and Design (Yorke 1999a: 18)

Whilst this student might have had a particularly poor experience of higher education, the responses from a number of ex-students in Art and Design suggest that, whilst they were not unhappy with their programme choices, they were unhappy with the programme they experienced (Yorke 1999b: 50–1). It was unclear whether these responses were representative of the student body in this subject area as a whole or whether they came from a particular subset of the students. One might ask whether the liberalism of pedagogic approach not unknown in this area was perceived by some students as casual and unsupportive. Engineering and Technology was another area in which teaching came in for criticism, but in this area programmes are typically heavily timetabled with 'contact hours' and hence the reasons for student disaffection are likely to have been quite different. Seymour and Hewitt (1997), in their extensive qualitative study of Science, Mathematics and Engineering in the US, provide evidence to suggest that the culture in these areas is not always optimally conducive to learning: it seems plausible that there might be some similarities in the UK. In contrast, responses from ex-students in Social Science, Humanities and Education were much less prone to cite dissatisfaction with the teaching of their programmes.

The pressures on academic staff to undertake research and consultancy, to engage with the community, and to involve themselves with institutional administrative activities such as quality assurance are well known. The availability of staff to students on an informal basis may, as a consequence, be constrained, as the following comment suggests:

> Academic staff, on occasions, had a tendency to project themselves as being very pushed for time, stressed out and could not fit you into their timetable of work. No matter who you turned to, or when you sought [*sic*] someone's aid, they seemed to be busy.
>
>   Student reading Science (Yorke 1999b: 40)

Some students were critical of the organization of their programmes. Where the programme followed by the student had two components, the articulation between them could break down:

> With my chosen degree having 2 parts, the organisation between the different [academic organizational units] was very poor. On several

occasions I was timetabled to be in 2 or 3 places at one time throughout the two years I was there.

Student reading for a joint honours degree in
Art and Design and Business (Yorke 1999a: 19)

Failure to cope with academic demand

Some students may simply fail to engage with their chosen programme. This could be interpreted in terms of poor choice in the first place, but might also reflect some lack of stimulation in the academic environment. Did the student who became bored by having only eight contact hours per week make a poor initial choice of programme, or did he simply not know how he should have responded to the demands made of him by his programme? If the latter, who should have been responsible for telling him?

Nearly one in three of the ex-students surveyed had been influenced in their withdrawal by a lack of sufficient academic progress. In some cases they had formally failed one or more programme components; in others the students had inferred that they were not going to make the grade and had withdrawn before the critical assessment point. Compared to the rest of the sample of 'non-completers', these students had found their programmes difficult and the workload too heavy, had felt they lacked the requisite study skills, and reported that they had suffered stress related to the programme.[80] Perhaps not surprisingly, these students were also more likely to have said that they made a poor choice of programme and that the student experience had been unsatisfactory. Sub-analyses of the data showed that the failure to cope with the demands of higher education was more prominent in science-based subject areas. Men cited more often than did women their lack of commitment to studying: weaknesses in study skills may have played a part here.

A disparity has been noted for some time between the performances of males and females in school education, and seems to have spread into higher education (Wolf 2003). Research into student progression and retention being conducted by Mark Prosser in the School of Biomolecular Sciences at Liverpool John Moores University is revealing a markedly different level of success between men and women, which does not seem to be attributable to standard background characteristics. Foster et al. (2002) have found a similar gender-related difference in performance at the University of Paisley.

Students did not always find support from their peers. A number of personal reasons were advanced, in which age and social class tended to predominate, for example:

Lack of involvement with other students on the course due to social class differences, being of a different class other students seemed to look down on me and refused to associate with me. Majority of other students came from southern England and disregarded people from the north of England.

Student reading Architecture (Yorke 1999a: 31)

I felt that being a middle class mature student did not help my integration into student life – I felt that my experience and knowledge put me on a different footing from other students. This meant that many seminars were inappropriate for me. [...] As I found it difficult to meet anyone of a similar age and background I did not enjoy the student way of life.

Student reading Arts (Yorke 1999a: 30)

Discordances in sexual orientation and in cultural background strongly influenced the withdrawal of two female students. One was a victim of homophobia:

These girls made my life hell with their petty immature comments and rumours. I have never before encountered homophobia except in this case. I could have done with more emotional support.

Student reading Science (Yorke 1999b: 16)

The other, from Northern Ireland, was ridiculed by both tutor and fellow students because she lacked a knowledge of the history of particular English towns. In her hall of residence, she

had to witness some form of acting between a few people who re-inacted [*sic*] boys standing against a wall and having their knees shot...

Student reading Social Science (Yorke 1999b: 16)

In such circumstances, withdrawal would seem to have been a highly rational action.

Extraneous and adventitious events

Higher education in the UK has been influenced considerably by two initiatives of the Labour government that took office in 1997. The first was the decision that students should contribute 'up front' to tuition fees,[81] with maintenance awards being replaced by loans. The second was the devolution of responsibility for higher education to authorities in Scotland, Wales and Northern Ireland, with that for higher education in England being retained by the Department for Education and Employment (now the Department for Education and Skills (DfES)). The two initiatives interacted, in that the different national authorities took different decisions regarding the fee contribution: Scotland, for instance, abolished the need for students to pay fee contributions 'up front' and replaced this by a charge consequent on graduation. More recently, the DfES (2003a) White Paper on higher education in England has proposed an increase in the fee contribution to a maximum of £3000 per year – the so-called 'top-up fee' coupled with income-contingent repayment.

The merits or otherwise of the changes to the funding of students are matters for consideration elsewhere. They have, however, accentuated the need for students to take up part-time employment in order to offset the costs of being a student, edging higher education towards the way in which students in the US, for a considerable time, and in Australia (more recently since the introduction and subsequent extension of the Higher Education Contribution Scheme (HECS)), have had to operate. The proportion of time students spend on part-time employment has been rising in the UK and Australia and has reached comparable levels in both countries – a mean, for such students, appears to be around 14 hours per week,[82] though ex-students responding to Davies and Elias' survey indicated that the mean for those who left in 1998–99 was 20 hours per week (Davies and Elias 2003: 61).[83]

As noted earlier, Yorke's (1999b) surveys took place before the UK policy changes on funding, yet at that time financial problems were a strong influence in the case of 37 per cent of respondents. For 15 per cent, the demands of employment whilst studying were influential. Approximately half of the respondents to Davies and Elias' (Davies and Elias 2003) study indicated that financial problems influenced their decision to withdraw. One in three of the first-year students surveyed by McInnis et al. (2000) who were considering withdrawing (these constituted roughly one-third of their original sample) indicated that finance was a factor in their thinking.

Some students panicked as they saw their level of debt rising:

> My main reason for leaving was finance. I soon realised that once I had paid my rent for the year, I would have no money left. Didn't want to leave the university owing '000s of £. So got a job.
>   Student reading Humanities (Yorke 1999b: 44)

Others stayed at home, but found the expense (financial and temporal) of travelling to their institution to have been unsustainably great. Advice was not always found, though responsibilities are divided between institutions (who need to make provision) and students (who, in general, need to take the initiative in seeking advice). A number of respondents to Davies and Elias' telephone survey noted that they had not received the help to which they felt they had been entitled (Davies and Elias 2003: 50). Four in ten of the respondents to the surveys led by Yorke had not discussed withdrawal with anyone in the institution (Yorke 1999b: 52), which is consistent with evidence from the focus groups in the NAO study (NAO 2002a: para. 2.8).

The tension between full-time study and part-time working is caught in the following:

> ... I was forced to work PT which ate into my studying time and my relaxation time. This generated a lot of stress for me ... My commitment to the course was affected. I didn't feel that studying an Art

degree subject with little career/job assurance justified the severe three-year struggle required to achieve it.

Student reading Art and Design (Yorke 1999b: 45)

There is some evidence (Barke et al. 2000) that academic achievements may be being adversely affected by part-time employment – certainly around half of the students from the University of Northumbria whom they surveyed felt this to be the case. The empirical evidence collected by Barke et al. (2000) is consistent with the students' beliefs: the mean percentage mark in year two for students engaging in part-time employment was calculated to be 3.6 percentage points (that is roughly one-third of an honours degree class) lower than that of their non-employed peers (Barke et al. 2000: 48).[84] The effect was stronger for male students than for females. If the evidence of Barke et al. is generalizable, then students engaging in part-time work are likely – explicitly or implicitly – to be trading off academic achievement against income generation.

For one student with dependants, the withdrawal may have had the silver lining of employment in an industry that was booming at the time:

As a mature-age student, I had a family to feed and a mortgage to pay. I had found part-time work in the evenings but this was not enough and when the chance to work full-time came along I took it.

Student reading Computing (Yorke 1999b: 45)

It is not only the academic programme that is significant in the choice process. The social and geographical environments may also have a significant impact on a student's willingness to persist on a programme of study. Someone from a quiet, perhaps rural, background may find a large city intimidating, and may not be sufficiently 'streetwise' to avoid trouble. Some environments – often those where students can find relatively inexpensive accommodation – are rough, as the following example illustrates:

In Feb '95 I was robbed at gunpoint close to the house I was living in. I was also burgled twice. Crime was a part of my life during my 1st year at the institution. It caused me to dislike the city – not the institution – and [I] decided it better to move to another institution.

Student reading Business (Yorke 1999b: 42)

On the other hand, a modestly-sized town proved a disappointment, as far as night life was concerned, for one student who found himself at a satellite campus instead of the main city campus of the institution in which he had enrolled. He had anticipated a city location, and felt that the institution concerned had misled him on this score.

Some students appear to have lacked the maturity to handle a new-found freedom, spending money and time on entertainment to the detriment of their academic studies. One appreciated, too late for remedy during his programme, that it would have been better if he had managed his life differently:

I was amazed by the 'big city'. I started clubbing regularly, took more and more drugs, became increasingly more ill, lost weight, became paranoid. I messed up in a very big way. One minute I was on top, the next rock bottom. I came from a cushioned background and believe if I had maybe waited a year or two and learnt more about the reality of life, then it would have been a different story.

Student reading joint Arts and Social Science (Yorke 1999a: 32)

Accidents, illnesses, homesickness and other extraneous causes all contribute to student withdrawal, but are beyond the power of an institution to rectify. However, an institution's approach to students who present problems of this kind will influence their return to higher education after a period of intercalation.

The withdrawal of part-time students

There is much less recent empirical evidence regarding the withdrawal of part-time students from programmes in higher education, not least because withdrawal is more difficult to index when there is no necessary expectation that students will be continuously engaged in study. Yorke's study did, however, obtain responses from 328 part-time students who had withdrawn from their programmes (mainly in new universities[85]), which were mainly in the areas of business and management, social sciences and healthcare. The top 12 influences on part-time students' decisions to withdraw are shown in Table 8.3. Given the limited and probably biased sample, the data need to be treated as suggestive rather than indicative.

Just over half of Yorke's sample of part-time respondents emphasized the demands of employment whilst studying as influential on their withdrawal, with around a quarter citing the needs of dependants, the weight of the workload and financial difficulty – matters that are likely to be inter-related. These part-time students were predominantly aged 25 or above, presumably with commitments outside higher education to match. Not surprisingly, the needs of dependants figured more strongly in the withdrawal of female students than in that of males. However, it is clear from Table 8.3 that part-time students are likely to be influenced in their withdrawal by factors that are markedly different from those precipitating withdrawal in their full-time and sandwich peers.

Around one-fifth of the respondents indicated that they were unhappy with one or more aspects of the programme as they experienced it. Many students (whether full-time or part-time) need support and encouragement from their tutors if they are to persist in their studies: the support may be expressed in task-related terms through comments on assignments and how improvement might be made, and also in more emotional terms that focus on the student as a person. In respect of the latter, how students perceive the way they are treated may be a significant factor: one wrote

Table 8.3   The top 12 influences on part-time students' withdrawal, compared with the levels of response given by full-time and sandwich students. (Data from Yorke 1999b: 59)

Influence	Percentage indicating moderate or considerable influence	
	PT (N = 328)	FT and SW (N = 2151)
Demands of employment whilst studying	52	15
Needs of dependants	26	15
Workload too heavy	25	17
Financial problems	23	37
Programme organization	22	27
Inadequate staff support outside timetable	21	24
Timetabling did not suit	21	11
Teaching did not suit me	19	31
Quality of teaching	19	23
Lack of personal support from staff	17	24
Personal health problems	17	23
Stress related to the programme	16	22

Part time students are treated like full time students, little sympathy or flexibility prevailed. Some tutors treated part time students like children.

Student reading Law (Yorke 1999b: 60)

Regrettably, retention and completion in respect of part-time study (which in 2001–2002 involved nearly 550,000 undergraduate students in the UK[86]) has attracted relatively little research attention since Bourner and colleagues' (1991) book (which contains a chapter on non-completion).[87] This is undoubtedly an area in which a call for further research ought to evoke a positive response from funding bodies.

9

Succeeding against the demographic odds

The policy context

We noted in Chapter 4 that, during the 1990s, retention and completion had become a significant policy issue in the UK and that, towards the end of this period, the Labour government had stressed its wish to increase the level of participation amongst groups that had hitherto been under-represented in higher education. It was, however, difficult to reconcile the tension between the desire to drive down the cost of student non-completion and the desire to enhance access amongst those groups which, as published statistics were to reveal clearly, would be at greatest risk of leaving their programmes before completing them.

As we pointed out in Chapter 5, press treatment of the institutional performance statistics over the years has demonstrated the inverse relationship between completion and access, with institutions being castigated or praised according to the value position of the particular newspaper. Political attention too has been strongly influenced by value positions, with some politicians slating institutions for poor completion whilst others have praised much the same institutions for their achievements in the field of access.

Optimizing institutional performance in terms of both access and completion is clearly important, for both political and more pragmatic reasons, and this chapter indicates how some institutions have responded to the challenge.

The performance of English[88] higher education institutions

The publication of statistics invites questions about the reasons for the patterns that the statistics appear to suggest. An inspection of the performance indicators published in 2000 (HEFCE 2000) showed that 28 English institutions were estimated to have levels of non-completion that were 'better' than those of the calculated benchmarks, and 14 institutions to have levels that were 'worse'[89] (Yorke 2001b). Of particular interest were the institutions that had performed 'better than benchmark' in terms of estimated non-completion, yet had student enrolments that were in demographic terms likely to be unfavourable to completion.[90] Was there something that these institutions were doing that enabled them to perform better than might have been expected, and from which useful lessons might be learned?

Investigating the correlates of institutional success[91]

Under its developmental programme 'Action on Access', HEFCE had been looking for ways in which widened participation in higher education could be followed by higher levels of completion than were the norm in English institutions. Yorke's (2001b) analysis provided the Action on Access team with a framework for responding to HEFCE's interest. However it was felt that, in that analysis, rather more weight was being given to the percentage of entrants from state schools than was merited, since there was no clear relationship between attendance at state schools and social class – there were, for example, many state schools that catered for primarily middle class pupils.[92] The decision was taken by the researchers[93] to focus attention on the six institutions which had non-completion performances flagged as superior to their benchmarks, and which had achieved these performances despite having at least one student demographic characteristic that was, across the sector, negatively correlated with completion.

The six institutions were:

- The University of Aston;
- The University of Lincolnshire and Humberside (now the University of Lincoln);
- Newman College of Higher Education;
- Sheffield Hallam University;
- Staffordshire University; and
- The University of Westminster.

Since the successes were visible at the level of the whole institution, it was decided to interview members of the senior management team whose roles bore upon the issue of student retention in order to determine what, if any, strategic approaches were being implemented. The interviews were conducted either on a one-to-one basis, or in small groups. The interviews led to two types of outcome: a general commentary on the features of institutions that seemed to be contributing to successful completion, and a series of vignettes (one for each institution) which captured some of the institution-specific details.[94]

A number of themes emerged which could plausibly be linked with the successful outcomes for students from lower socio-economic groups, although some institutional managers seemed to have difficulty in pinning down the reasons for their institutions' success. Some factors that bear on student success cannot, of course, be influenced by institutions. For example, Thomas et al. (2001) noted that the provision of public transport may be inadequate to permit those students who do not have access to a vehicle to attend an institution, and in areas of particular deprivation some people are reluctant to leave their homes unattended because of fears that they will be subjected to vandalism and burglary.

Influences on student success

A student-centred approach

The strongest feature of the six institutions (only one of which was an old university) was a sustained commitment to a broad conception of 'the student experience'. There was an emphasis on teaching in a majority of these institutions, with research appearing as an important but subsidiary commitment. In one institution it was explained that teaching and learning had always been its primary focus, and that there had not been a strong culture of research, although a recent commitment to raising the profile of research might be about to result in a shift in institutional priorities. In a second, a high proportion of the academic staff was teacher trained, giving them a general appreciation of pedagogy and learning. Whilst there was strong encouragement to undertake research, the institution's mission focused unambiguously upon high-quality teaching and the effective support of student learning.

A third institution had taken a more wide-ranging approach to the student experience that was almost 'total quality' in manner, by actively involving the full range of its staff in supporting students. Training activities underpinned this commitment. When a student was perceived by any member of staff to be in some sort of difficulty, it was expected that this would be followed through in an appropriate way: housekeeping staff in a hall of residence, for example, knew how to refer students to sources of support. The commitment of this institution to the development of its students, and the attention it gave to teaching, had to some extent shaped its research effort.

In all of the interviews, the view was expressed that students quickly became known in the institution as individuals. This led to a sense of 'belonging' in the institution (or, in the larger institutions, in the relevant part of the institution). The 'friendliness' of the institution was often suggested as a reason for relatively high levels of student engagement. However, student engagement was more problematic where the institution was spread over a number of sites relatively distant from each other, since the 'non-home' sites could be perceived by students – with perhaps a touch of exaggeration – as alien territory.

Pre-entry and early engagement with students

All of the institutions engaged in outreach work with potential entrants, which included work with primary and secondary schools, with colleges and to a lesser extent with community groups. There were three main purposes: to demystify higher education for those who had no previous connection with it, and hence to build an awareness of what entry had to offer; to begin the process of engagement with the institution; and to prepare aspiring entrants for the demands of academic study. One institution had made a particular point of developing 'key skills' in students before they arrived. A second had, as a move towards the smoothing of entry, introduced 'year zero' courses in some subjects at a local further education college. A third institution had made pre-entry communication a strong feature of its provision, sending students newsletters, e-mails and text messages.

At enrolment time, teams of students dressed in highly recognizable T-shirts were typically recruited to act as informal mentors for queries regarding where things could be found, what needed to be done, and so on. This was felt not only to be a good thing in its own right (and not least because near-peers were involved), but also a contribution to the development in students of a sense of engagement with the institution.

Curricular matters

The political pressure to widen participation in UK higher education had had its impact on the curricula running in the six institutions. The institutions had responded in different ways, reflecting their particular circumstances. Claims were made by respondents of changes to aspects of provision such as the following: curriculum content; the accreditation of skills gained through part-time employment; approaches to teaching; the ways in which staff were expected to provide tutorial support; modes of assessment; flexibility with respect to student circumstances (such as in respect of attendance and of assessment deadlines); and the opportunities for repeating courses and assessments.

Curriculum development had, in one institution, involved the creation and delivery of programmes of diverse interest and significance, such as

Islamic Studies and Black Music Studies. It argued that the introduction of programmes such as these had both direct and indirect virtues. The programmes were not only directly attractive to potential students, but also they were indirectly attractive in that they signalled to different groups that the institution valued the cultures and achievements of a wide range of groups in a diverse society.

Bringing social and academic engagement closer

Tinto's (1993) model indicates that social engagement, as well as academic engagement, is an important influence on student retention. One institution had implicitly, if not explicitly, acknowledged the point and was exploring ways in which teaching and learning could be made more interactive and social, for example by introducing more group work into learning activities, and by creating within the traditionally silent library and learning resource centre spaces in which discussion was allowed. Developments such as these may be particularly significant where students spend limited time at the institution because of the need to take part-time employment in order to help them pay their way through higher education.

The first year experience

Induction into the institution appeared to be an important process within each of the six institutions, and usually extended beyond the traditional period of up to a week. One made a specific point of inducting students into the academic discourse of higher education, which helped in the preparation of students for the academic demands to be made upon them. Another had developed a virtual learning environment (VLE) whose purpose was to help students from a wide range of backgrounds to come to terms with the demands of higher education. Students were required to engage with the VLE, on an independent basis, and to follow a personalized study programme. This strategy had been adopted in order to ensure that all first year students developed both the academic and computer-related skills that were necessary to succeed in higher education, without those from disadvantaged backgrounds being placed at risk of stigmatization. Instead of providing separate study skills modules, a third had decided to contextualize 'key skills' by incorporating them into normal subject modules. A fourth had decided to place careers education early in the first semester, on the grounds that this could help students to appreciate the range of opportunities potentially open to them post-graduation (and indirectly reinforcing the utility-value of the chosen programme of study).

One institution had for some years acknowledged the importance of the whole of the first year to student persistence, by prioritizing the first year in its resource allocations and by offsetting the extra early costs with savings in subsequent years. The underlying principle was that a 'pay-off' in the longer term could accrue from an early investment in developing students' capacity to learn independently.

Assessment

In most of the institutions there appeared to have been a shift away from early summative assessments in favour of formative assessment. This seemed to be reflecting the view that summative assessments early in a study programme could lead to unnecessary failure because some students had simply not had sufficient time to come to terms with the demands of higher education. Such students were felt to be more likely to benefit from formative assessment than from having to re-take a failed study unit (an issue discussed further in Chapter 10). Some early assessments had been made summative in the limited sense that the student was required to make an attempt at them, but the weighting given to the awarded grade was either zero or sufficiently low as not to prejudice later retrieval.

One institution had recognized that students who carried first year failures into the subsequent year would suffer from an excessive academic workload. It had therefore developed revision summer schools in a couple of subject areas in order to allow the students an early opportunity to retrieve their position and hence to facilitate progression.

Personal tutoring

Most institutions had recently re-introduced or revised their personal tutor systems, in recognition that the assumptions of the past (often given only a token reality in practice) were unsustainable as both resources and students' presence on campus became more constrained. The personal tutor was seen as potentially one of the stable points of contact between student and institution. One approach that had been adopted was based on much tighter guidelines for students and staff about the purpose and contents of tutorials. Another institution had extended the idea in moving to introduce tutorials that were based upon an agenda that the student was required to prepare in advance.

Student finance and related issues

In most of the institutional discussions, finance and related issues were raised as a significant disincentive to student persistence in higher education. Three main approaches had been adopted by the institutions: to provide information and guidance about financial matters; to make available direct financial support; and to facilitate part-time employment.

Institutions sought to help their students to take a balanced and informed approach to debt, and were offering information about the sources of finance that were available and how to apply for funding. Finance was, however, noted as being a particularly sensitive matter, with some students being averse to 'debt counselling', as well as to debt itself.

In all the institutions a limited number of government-funded bursaries were available to students from low-income backgrounds, but the perception was that the value of these was set too low. HEFCE provided institutions with hardship funds on a per capita basis and, although these were used to the full, it was felt that more students ought to be able to benefit from them. Some dissatisfaction was expressed that the national guidelines precluded some deserving students from benefiting from these funds. Further, it was reported that some students could not gain access to this source of support because they had not taken out a student loan beforehand,[95] and – separately – that perceptions of possibly being stigmatized were causing students not to apply. Institutions also typically held small, self-generated funds which they could use for purposes such as the provision of emergency support.

There was a pragmatic acceptance in all of the institutions that many students – especially those from lower socio-economic groups – needed to undertake part-time employment in order to provide the resources needed for them to complete their programmes of study. However, it was recognized that some students chose to earn money in order to enable them to fulfil lifestyle ambitions that might not meet with middle-class approval.[96] Institutions had found ways of supporting part-time employment, such as by employing some students within the institution[97] (and thereby signalling to students that the institution was not hostile to part-time employment), and by facilitating part-time working via 'jobshops' and employment agencies. In some circumstances the institution exercised a measure of control over the students' part-time employment.

Staff development and research

The interviews found examples of staff development activity being employed to facilitate the changes in teaching and learning practices that were deemed to be necessary if the needs of a more diverse student cohort were to be fulfilled. One institution had an institution-wide network devoted to the sharing of relevant good practice, which was claimed to be both popular and effective. Another had created a 'best practice' unit. Two of the six institutions had dedicated research units that specialized in higher education and supported the improvement of institutional policies and practices by focusing on issues relevant to staff development and/or the widening of participation.

Other approaches to success

The political pressure for the widening of access to higher education had strengthened since this project was completed in 2001, and there was a comparable increase in interest in what institutions were, and could be, doing in order to maximize the success of students who – the performance statistics showed – were less likely to complete their programmes of study.

The contacts that Action on Access had with the English higher education sector indicated that many institutions with high proportions of students who were older and/or from the lower socio-economic groups were making considerable efforts to provide a supportive environment, even if this had not yet been reflected in the national retention and completion statistics. HEFCE saw the potential to build up a compendium of practice that could have transfer-value, and funded the work through Action on Access.[98] Nine institutions with appropriate demographic characteristics agreed to participate in the study, which involved interviews with a wider range of senior staff and, in the majority of cases, with one or more student representatives.

The nine institutions were:

- Bolton Institute;
- University of Bradford;
- University of Central Lancashire;
- Chester College of Higher Education;
- University of Derby;
- University of East London;
- Edge Hill College of Higher Education;
- University of Salford; and
- University of Wolverhampton.

A similar semi-structured interview format was used, this time reflecting the student life-cycle (aspiration raising; pre-entry support; welcoming and induction; on-course support; and employability) which had recently emerged (HEFCE 2001b), and concentrating attention on the middle three phases.

Aspiration raising and pre-entry support

There were a number of ways in which institutions were working to encourage entry into higher education and to help students meet the challenges associated with the transition. Amongst these were outreach work with potential students from disadvantaged environments; close links between further education and some of the higher education institutions (which could extend to the guaranteeing of entry if appropriate conditions were met); and special programmes designed to orient incoming students –

especially those coming from backgrounds with little or no exposure to higher education – to the demands likely to be made of them.

Welcoming and induction

The importance of the students' first experience of the higher education institution was widely acknowledged. Students could, if they found the institution unwelcoming, simply leave or, alternatively, move to a different institution if the opportunity arose.[99]

In some institutions, approaches to induction had been implemented that went beyond the 'freshers' week' of orientation to academic departments, institutional services and student societies and facilities. The induction process was extended or enhanced, and one had taken the view that the first year experience could, *in toto*, be treated as an induction into the honours part of the degree programme.[100] Use was made in some institutions of diagnostic testing in order to assess the needs students might have in respect of study skill support.

Student support services had been reorganized in a number of institutions along 'one stop shop' lines, so that students could find out, by contacting a single source of information or 'portal', where they needed to go to gain access to the service they required. In at least one institution, support services were introduced through social activities involving peers. In another, the careers service had taken the initiative to mail incoming students to inform them of what it was able to offer, and had noted early uptake to have risen as a result (it had been found that students often contacted the careers service too late in their academic studies to derive maximum benefit from what was available).

On-course support

Institutions had made various changes to their curricular provision in order to respond to the needs of their students. Some had introduced 'learning to learn' (or similar) provision into the first year curriculum. The role of the personal tutor was re-emerging as significant, as institutions sought to combat the impersonality of the student experience that was particularly associated with programmes that had high enrolments. There were examples of web-based materials being used, with the staff 'contact time' being restructured into supportive tutorials. Support services in most institutions had developed new approaches to students, involving workshops and other activities targeted on particular aspects of need, such as the development of study skills and of numeracy, and the provision of summer schools designed to help those faced with having to re-take some of their assessments. A significant change was the trend (noted in the earlier project) towards formative assessment in the first semester, in recognition that it was not ideal from a developmental point of view to burden struggling students with the additional demand of re-taking assessments.[101]

Employability

Students in some of the institutions had the opportunity to mentor others, not only helping their less experienced peers to develop their sense of engagement in higher education but also strengthening their own curricula vitae (resumes) in respect of employment. They thus helped peers to persist whilst they enhanced their own chances of success (broadly construed). In some institutions, students can gain academic credit through acting as representatives and reflecting on what they have done, and also acquire the less tangible credit that potential employers might ascribe to work which shows that they have exercised a measure of responsibility for others. A number of student unions were actively engaged in initiatives of these kinds. In some institutions the providers of student services were involved in the arranging of part-time employment for students.

Influences on student success

Although the two sets of interviews arose from different research questions which were pursued through rather different interview methodologies, some general themes emerge from the mass of qualitative detail that was generated by the two studies. An *institutional* commitment to student success was vital if successes were not to be limited to those parts of the institution in which such a commitment ran high. This institutional commitment appeared to be strengthened when any or all of the following conditions obtained.

- The institutional climate was perceived by students as supportive and 'friendly'.
- There was an institutional emphasis on support from both academic departments and the support services leading up to, and during, the first year of study.
- There was an emphasis on formative assessment in the early stage of a programme.
- The importance of the social dimension was recognized in the provision of learning activities.
- There was an acceptance of the fact that the pattern of students' engagement in higher education was changing, and this was accompanied by a preparedness to respond positively to this in various ways.

The first year of full-time study is critically important for retention. If students can come to terms with the demands of higher education during their first year, then the odds are strongly in favour of their completing their programme of study. Hence there is a logic to the disproportionation of resource allocations in favour of the first year experience.

The chances of success in higher education are strengthened if students have the cultural capital that enables them to make the transition into higher education relatively easily. Students with no familial exposure to higher education are at a disadvantage, since they have less access to tacit knowledge about expectations and procedures than those whose families have engaged in higher education. Pre-entry bridging programmes can be helpful in this respect, and some of the institutions visited during the course of the two studies were able to provide statistical evidence that these had been successful in enhancing retention.

An institution that is perceived as 'friendly' will probably be successful in providing, through its academic and support staff, the emotional and practical sustenance that those from disadvantaged backgrounds (especially, but not exclusively) are likely to need. The level of success is likely to be enhanced where the institution establishes a climate in which the staff collectively demonstrate a commitment to the students – this needs to be a matter of practice and not mere rhetoric.

Formative assessment can be a powerful influence on learning. Black and Wiliam (1998) conducted a meta-analysis of a large number of studies of formative assessment (mainly in school environments, though their sample did include some from higher education), and found that the statistical 'size effect' was considerable. It is probably not unreasonable to extrapolate their findings broadly across higher education, with the caveat that the feedback given needs to take a number of factors into account (Yorke 2003a) and needs to assist the student to undertake subsequent tasks, that is, be useful in developmental terms (Knight 2002). Formative assessment is vital in the early stages of a programme, especially when students are coming to terms with demands that are different from those that they have previously experienced. Programmes in which summative assessments appear at the end of the first semester may not allow sufficient time for the student to acclimatize to higher education, nor for adequate formative assessment to take place, with the consequence that some students perform less well than they might have done, perhaps to the extent of suffering the additional burden of 'failing and trailing' modules (Yorke 2001a). Educationally, it is undesirable to have a curriculum structure that does not allow students sufficient scope to learn from formative assessment and that, as a consequence, prejudices the continuation of study.

Lastly, the opportunities provided by information and communications technology should not distract attention from the social side of the higher education experience. A lot of learning occurs through social interactions of various kinds, and – taking for the moment an instrumental slant – employers consistently say that they require graduates who are good at various forms of social exchange, such as knowing how to encourage people to undertake tasks, or operating successfully as a member of a team. Where students live at home whilst studying and/or spend time in part-time employment, the opportunities for engaging in the social side of the higher education experience are constrained. Hence it becomes important that the time formally allocated to a programme is not only used to address the social expectations of potential employers and of life in general, but also to foster a sense of 'belonging' in the institution.

10

Promoting student success

Overview

In Chapter 8 it was suggested that there were four broad categories of influence on students' withdrawal from their programmes:

- Flawed decision-making about entering the programme;
- Students' experience of the programme and the institution generally;
- Failure to cope with the demand of the programme; and
- Events that impact on students' lives outside the institution.

In this chapter we discuss ways in which the likelihood of withdrawal might be minimized – and hence the chances of success might be maximized. We subdivide the discussion into what institutions can do (the primary focus of this book), what students can do, and what a higher education system might do. We approach these issues from a UK perspective, realizing that adjustments may be needed in respect of other national higher education systems. Our engagement with relevant theoretical constructs (especially in Chapter 6) ought to facilitate the transferability of what we have to say.[102]

What should be the focus?

Before we get into the practicalities, we need to emphasize that to focus on maximizing retention risks mistaking symptom for cause. A policy focus on student success in higher education through teaching, learning and assessment, and through institutional support services, is likely to lead to better retention than a focus on retention itself. Tinto (1993: 145ff) puts forward three principles of effective retention which can be boiled down to a commitment to students, their education, and their integration into the institution's social and educational community. He then adds seven principles of effective implementation which relate to programme development and the coherence of institutional activities in support of retention.

Those with a background in quality assurance will see, in Tinto's principles, principles of quality enhancement as applied to the needs of the student. Tinto leaves it to institutions to interpret and operationalize the principles in the light of local circumstances.

In a special issue of the *Journal of College Student Retention*, Braxton and Mundy (2001) take a more operational perspective on retention, listing 47 recommendations (44 of which are held to be consistent with Tinto's principles) which draw on suggestions made by a number of contributors.[103] These recommendations range between the specific (for example '*Student Affairs offices should conduct workshops on coping with stress*') and the general (for example '*Consistently use good practices in teaching, learning, and retention programs*'). The recommendations are, not surprisingly, coloured by their applicability to higher education in the US, and some will need to be 'translated' to take into account other contexts.

An emphasis on retention, however, implicitly puts the institutional interest to the fore, since it is at root a 'supply-side' construct. This can be rationalized to some extent by asserting that retention is 'a good thing' for students, but the connotations of institutional performance remain. However, a focus on student success unambiguously places the students' interest centre stage.

This is, of course, not to deny that a focus on retention has merit. Tinto (1993) points out that an institutional focus on retention can lead to appraisal of curricular and pedagogic matters – as it has done with conspicuous success, for example at Napier University (see Chapter 5; Johnston 2003). The Open University has a retention programme which demonstrates how a concern for retention interfaces with a range of aspects of the student experience, and points out a number of risks to student persistence that – with some forethought – can be reduced (HEFCE 2001b: 36ff).

In what follows, we offer a number of points for consideration whilst acknowledging that institutions will have addressed at least some already, perhaps in response to the expectations of external quality scrutiny undertaken by national agencies and accrediting bodies – and perhaps also with an eye to the publication of performance data and (for those at the extremes of the distributions) the consequent attention of the press (as Chapter 5 showed). To focus on student success is, implicitly, to focus on the enhancement of the quality of the student experience. In what we offer can be seen a marked relationship with the kinds of educational principle advocated by writers such as Chickering and Gamson (1987) and Tinto (1993).

What can be done to enhance the chances of student success?

This question, the up-side of that relating to minimizing student attrition, can be answered in many ways. Some matters are primarily under institutional control, whereas others are for students to take in hand. Yet others are matters beyond the powers of institutions or individuals, and are the responsibility of higher education systems. We have divided our suggestions in this tripartite manner, giving our main attention to the ways in which institutions can maximize the chances that their students will succeed.

Our suggestions are influenced by the theoretical and empirical literature, though the complexity of the topic often makes it difficult to make simple connections between the literature and institutional practice. The suggestions are general rather than specific: some are, frankly, commonsense. Whilst it would have been possible to construct a detailed list of possible actions, the specificity of these would ill-fit a diverse higher education system, let alone the greater international diversity of higher education systems. We therefore leave it to readers to determine how our suggestions might be applied to local circumstances – that is, to apply the European Union's principle of 'subsidiarity'.

What institutions can do

Improving student decision-making regarding programmes

Whilst much of the responsibility for deciding on a programme belongs to the intending student, there are actions that institutions can take to help.

1. *Make as much information as possible available.* The UK National Audit Office suggested that applicants needed information on course content; methods of assessment; work placements; expected time-commitment; ancillary costs; success rates of past students; and employment destinations (NAO 2002a: para. 4.2). What is curiously missing from this list, especially in the light of Yorke's (1999b) findings, is the quality of the student experience. As well as prospectuses, institutions make available specific programme information, organize open days, and offer the opportunity to visit the relevant department on a more individual basis. On its website,[104] UCAS makes available to potential applicants '*Entry Profiles*' for programmes run in UK institutions. These are of varying informativeness, but do contain links to reports from the Quality Assurance Agency on the quality of provision. One of the more informative Entry Profiles is that for the BSc (Hons) Geography at the University of Manchester which, in addition to addressing the issue of

entry requirements, provides students with answers to the questions *'What can this course offer me?'* and *'Is this course right for me?'*, which could be followed up in greater depth in a visit to the university. It is probably only when an intending student visits an institution that they can establish whether the programme and institution are likely to be 'right' for them.[105]

2. *Make that information welcoming to the full range of potential students.* Whilst significant improvements have been made to publicity material in respect of the representation of gender and ethnicity, there is probably a need for further attention to be given to age and disability. Read et al. (2003: 265), for example, found from extensive focus group research that 'a number of mature students noted their sense of alienation when reading the university's prospectus', seeing it as implicitly stressing the facilities available for young people. The corollary of producing broadly welcoming materials is that this has to be followed through in institutional practices.

3. *Recruit students who have a realistic chance of succeeding.* The pressure on institutions to meet financial targets, coupled with the removal of the 'cap' on institutional numbers in England, means that institutions towards the lower end of the reputational range are tempted to open their doors to a wider range of students than hitherto. Widening participation without thinking through the implications for student success is likely to be followed by poor retention. This is not to suggest that an institution should 'play safe' by recruiting students with normative entry qualifications (that would close down educational opportunities), but playing safe is a temptation wherever retention data are used to judge institutional performance. Attention needs to be given to the 'fit' of students with what the institution has to offer. It also needs to be given to the induction of students into the expectations and practices of higher education, the provision of appropriate programmes, and the adoption of appropriate pedagogic and support strategies.

4. *Advise students according to the students' best interests, not the institution's.* It does neither party any long-term good to encourage students to enrol on programmes which may be unsuitable – for example, to downplay the importance of qualifications in Mathematics for programmes in Engineering. The norm of an Honours Degree programme may not be the best initial option, as some withdrawn students discovered (Davies and Elias 2003: 39). For some potential students in England and Northern Ireland, for example, a two-year full-time Foundation Degree[106] may be more suitable (with the option to transfer subsequently to an Honours Degree), or a 'gap year' may be the most appropriate course of action (as a number of respondents acknowledged in response to the survey conducted by Davies and Elias 2003).

The student experience

Choy (2002), reviewing research on three federally-sponsored longitudinal studies in the US, concluded that factors positively influencing persistence and completion included the following:

- A rigorous precursor programme of studies in high school;
- Limiting the number of hours of employment whilst studying in college; and
- Having parents who had gained at least a bachelor's degree.

With the possible exception of the second, these are beyond the reach of the higher education institution. However, the data on the persistence of non-traditional students led Choy to suggest that attention to the first-year experience might lead to improved retention and completion. Like Tinto (1993) and many others, we take the view that institutions are likely to maximize their students' chances of success if they pay particular attention to the first year experience.

General

5. *Adopt a welcoming attitude to students.* This applies as much when students are choosing the programmes on which they will enrol as when they arrive at the institution. An offhand approach, disorganized or overly bureaucratic arrangements, and excessive queuing for activities are all inimical to student engagement. In Chapter 9 evidence was presented that a positive approach to students, supported by existing students as guides and mentors to newcomers, can help students to feel at home in the institution.[107] Pelling (2001) stresses the importance of mentoring and peer support for students from 'non-traditional' groups and the sensitivity with which this has to be handled, especially when those involved come from different racial backgrounds.

6. *Acknowledge that higher education is, at heart, a social process.* Distance learning might be regarded as an exception, but for distance-learning students the social aspect is conducted through various media. Considerable weight is placed nowadays on resource-based learning, and this can be both an effective and an efficient contribution to student learning. For most students, though, it is the exchanges with tutors and peers (however mediated) that indicate to them the quality of their learning. The risk is that 'packaged learning' (a contradiction in terms) may not be complemented by the level of tutorial support that students need if they are to engage fully with their work. The social process may be affected by students' perception that the institution is the right one for them to be in (some of the examples in Chapter 8 are consistent with Bourdieu's conception of the reproduction of social structure).

7. *Engage with students before they actually arrive.* In addition to providing information (preferably in a 'user-friendly' format), it may be a good idea to set up some form of pre-entry workshop or course which will help students to become oriented to the institution and to the demands that higher education will make of them (NAO 2002a: para. 5.2). This is particularly relevant for those students who enter higher education from backgrounds other than that of having recently taken A Levels at school, and can be effective, as is exemplified by Abramson and Jones' (2003) work at the University of Central Lancashire. In some cultures, engagement with the *parents and guardians* of young students is important, particularly where there is no familial background of higher education. This can assist parents and guardians in supporting students through the transition into, and continuation in, higher education.[108]

8. *Make the induction process welcoming and effective.* Avoid the overloading of students with information: concentrate on the essentials, but have a system through which students can follow up particular personal needs. For Honours Degree programmes in England, Wales and Northern Ireland it is not unreasonable to think of the whole of the first year of full-time study (or its part-time equivalent) in terms of an extended induction to Honours level study. Draw on existing students as sources of local – in more than one sense – knowledge: they can provide a slant on provision and the environment that may be lacking from the official sources of information. The use of highly visible T-shirts helps such students to be recognized.

9. *Have, as far as possible, a 'one-stop shop' or a portal for support services.* This maximizes the possibility that a student's query or problem can quickly be brought to the attention of someone who may be able to help, and eliminates the need for the student to scurry from one office to another, sometimes in very different locations, and becoming demoralized. The existence of a 'one-stop shop' was noted in institutions that were making considerable effort to enhance student success (Yorke and Thomas 2003), and the connection of support services to retention is addressed more generally in UUK (2002b).

10. *Encourage students to feel that they belong in the institution.* For some students, a sense of belonging will develop as a matter of course; for others this may not happen unless the institution makes an effort. A range of writers, including Tinto (1993), Mentkowski and Associates (2000) and Read et al. (2003), have in various ways emphasized the importance to a student of feeling that they are a member of a community. Kuh (nd: 1) sums up a wealth of experience in the US when he says: 'Those institutions that more fully engage their students in the variety of activities that contribute to valued outcomes of college can claim to be of higher quality than [others] ...' However, 'engagement' may take a different profile for the 18-year-old residential student than for, say, the mature commuter student with commitments to dependants.

11. *Help students to become 'streetwise' in their environment.* Students who know

the city or town in which they are studying will generally be aware of areas in which they need to be particularly careful in looking after themselves and their belongings. 'Outsiders' may be less aware, and the institution – probably in conjunction with the students' union – can help them to prevent the burglary of flats and also attacks in street locations, such as at cash dispensers (Barberet et al. 2003).

12. *Support the development of expertise in teaching.* Teaching has to compete with other activities (quintessentially research) of academics. There is a 'homeostatic' tendency for academics to reproduce the teaching experiences with which they are familiar, which may not lead to the engagement of students in more active forms of learning. The availability of materials in electronic form means that 'transmissive' forms of teaching, such as lecturing, need to be used judiciously, rather than unquestioningly. Contact between academics and students needs to be characterized as 'quality time', in which the expensive resource of the former needs to be used to optimal effect. The more learning experiences are 'active', the greater is the chance of student engagement. An institutional commitment to student learning implies a sustained commitment to the promotion of teaching approaches likely to enhance students' success, and requires firm leadership.

Academic

13. *Provide a culture supportive of student learning.* Seymour and Hewitt (1997) provide a number of examples of cultures in science-based departments that were indifferent to, and in some instances inimical to, student learning. Wherever there is pressure on academics to focus on tasks other than student learning, there is a risk that the academic culture will be perceived by students as indifferent to their needs. Where students perceive indifference, there may be an effect on students' engagement, and, as Astin (1993: 382) observes, his data 'support the argument that the student's academic and personal development can be enhanced by heavy involvement'. A corollary is that the setting of expectations regarding academic studies should occur very early in students' experience, otherwise students might 'get off on the wrong foot' (as used to be the case with early 'rag weeks' in higher education in the UK).

14. *Ensure that programme structures are conducive to student success.* It might be felt that to make the point is unnecessary, since the procedures for programme approval should have addressed the issue. However, as was noted earlier in respect of the first year experience, the use of summative assessment at the end of the first semester (when many students will still be finding their feet in higher education) may act against student success. Student learning does not necessarily fit neatly into the compartments (modules and the like) into which the curriculum is

subdivided, and may take the whole programme to come to fruition: some aspects of employability, such as dealing with interpersonal situations, fall into this category. Programme structures need to accommodate such 'slow learning' (Claxton 1998), since some aspects of student success depend on it. In his study of Seattle Community College, Tinto (1997) demonstrated the importance of students having coherence in their studies rather than taking a disconnected set of modules – in modular schemes in the UK, it is typical for students to follow 'routes' which include a set of core modules.

15. *Ensure that the teaching approaches adopted are conducive to student success.* As well as attending to disciplinary understandings and to the development of skilful practices within and outwith the discipline, there is a need to attend to the development of metacognitive and self-regulatory capacity, and to 'emotional intelligence'. Attention to metacognition has been shown by Marzano (1998) in a large meta-analytic study to be a powerful contribution to knowledge gain, and has the potential to influence student performance across the full gamut of life-experience. Further, a similar statistical size-effect was found to apply when the experimental intervention focused on the student's self-system, which makes a connection with the theoretical and empirical work of researchers such as Dweck (1999) and Bandura (1997). Developing students' 'self' in a number of respects has the potential for enhancing success later in programmes. The provision of 'quality time' for teacher-student interaction and formative assessment are key components here. Schutte and Malouff (2002), drawing on Goleman's (1996) work on 'emotional intelligence', found that the inclusion of 'emotional skills' in first semester courses in a private university in the south-eastern US led to an enhanced ability to recognize, regulate and harness emotions, and also to better persistence, than was the case with students not receiving emotionally-themed courses.[109]

16. *Make good use of formative assessment.* The rise of modular schemes in UK higher education has been accompanied by an emphasis on summative assessment at the expense of formative assessment. Knight and Yorke (2003) argue that greater attention needs to be paid to formative assessment – not only because much summative assessment cannot bear the weight of expectation laid upon it, but more importantly because of the capacity of formative assessment to enhance student learning.[110] The previous discussion strongly implies that formative assessment needs to be constructive and supportive, encouraging the adoption of learning goals, if maximum benefit is to be gained by the student. It also needs to be used early in programmes, so that students begin to appreciate what higher education will be expecting of them – which may be rather different from what may have been expected in other forms of education.

17. *Disproportionate the allocation of resources in favour of the first year experience.* The argument, made by Tinto (1993) and others, and implemented by

Sheffield Hallam University apparently to good effect (Yorke 2003a), is that, if students can be encouraged to develop their independence as learners at the beginning of their programmes, the initial investment of resources will pay for itself in later years of study. This runs counter to practice in some institutions, in which final year work is characterized, *inter alia*, by smaller teaching groups and hence a higher resource/student ratio.

Failure to cope with the demand of the programme

18. *Respond to students' pre-existing level of knowledge.* This is as much a programme design issue as a teaching and learning issue. Ausubel (1968) asserted that teachers needed to start from the student's current level of knowledge. Where students enter programmes from a variety of backgrounds, the pitching of the level of material is clearly problematic, since the assumption of a common platform of understanding is unlikely to be tenable. Some diagnostic activity is likely to be helpful, but it needs to be supported by materials and learning experiences that can quickly help students fill in the gaps in their understanding. This could take place in a pre-entry workshop[111] or during an orientation session at the beginning of the first semester. However, it takes time, which could cause problems in semesterized programmes in which summative assessment at the end of the first semester is strongly weighted.

19. *Ensure that students know what is expected of them.* Students may enter higher education with misperceptions of what is expected of them, and so it is wise to make clear at the outset what is expected, and to back that up with exercises early in the programme that can act as vehicles for informing students whether their approach to their work is appropriate. Study support services and student mentors can be helpful in this respect.

20. *Use formative assessment early in the programme.* The point was made earlier, but can be extended here to note that the important issue is to ensure that feedback consists not only of comments on the submitted work, but also helps the student to make a better job of future assignments (Boud 1995; Knight 2002).

21. *Treat academic failure as a developmental opportunity.* One virtue of the often-maligned competency approach to education has been the distinction between 'competent' and 'not yet competent', in contrast to that between passing and failing. A 'not yet competent' perspective on failure implies the possibility of success further on, provided the cause(s) of failure are understood and appropriate action is undertaken. As with withdrawal in general, failure can be influenced by many factors, singly or in combination. These include an inadequate grasp of the subject matter, a misperception of what was expected, 'exam nerves', wrong choice of programme in the first place, and a lifestyle

unattuned to learning. Rogers (2002: 113) differentiates between interim and terminal failure, pointing out that the former 'needs to be understood as an unavoidable and perhaps necessary part of the learning process'. Academic failure at one point in time need not be construed by the student as catastrophe and, through its various channels of support, the institution may be in a position to help the student to see their failure in interim, rather than terminal, terms and to envision how it might be converted into success.

Events that impact on students' lives outside the institution

22. *Appreciate the complexity of pressures on contemporary students.* Whilst institutions widely acknowledge that students have to make trade-offs between competing demands, the actual treatment of students may belie this (see, for example, the case of the mature Law student, noted in Chapter 8, who found no sympathy in respect of family and travel difficulties).
23. *Respond sympathetically to adventitious events in students' lives.* Accidents, criminal attacks and illnesses, for example, strike without warning, disrupting a student's engagement in study. A period of intercalation may be needed by the student, but it may not really be necessary for the student to restart the year (as sometimes is required by the letter of the institutional law). Other students may simply need some money to tide them over a short-term difficulty, or need help with the financing of childcare: institutions in the UK typically have a limited amount of money available for such purposes.
24. *Invite potential withdrawers to an exit interview.* This can lead to students discovering that withdrawal may not be the inevitable course of action that they envisaged.

A note on institutional culture

Kuh (2001–2002) warns against an uncritical acceptance of the power of institutional culture to influence academic outcomes. He points out that, where the student body is diverse, some groups will be more comfortable than others with that espoused by the institution. Discomfort may, however, lead to lower or higher levels of success: some students may be alienated and depart whereas others exploit their alienation through forming (or joining) a counter-cultural group and thereby succeed. Running through Kuh's discussion is a socio-cultural strand the late Pierre Bourdieu would have recognized. What is missing from Kuh's account (probably because of his focus on the institution) are the sub-cultures of the institution: academic departments are key influences here, and can create their own cultural 'islands' within the larger institution. Media Studies, for example, is a relatively youthful academic area in UK institutions that has had to assert its right to join longer established areas, and group solidarity amongst academics and students helped it to acquire academic acceptance.

Acknowledging Kuh's points, there is some evidence that institutional culture has the potential to – and can – influence student success. Strong institutional commitments that bear in various ways on student success are in evidence at the following, for example:

- Alverno College, which has had a sustained commitment to eight broad 'abilities' at progressively more complex levels in both general education and the specialist subject(s), and emphasizes formative assessment (Mentkowski and Associates 2000).
- Indiana University – Purdue University, Indianapolis, which has developed 'a core set of Principles of Undergraduate Learning that guide the development of program curriculum, the evaluation of program effectiveness, and the development of student proficiencies ...' (Borden and Evenbeck 2003).
- The University of Sydney, which allocates a proportion of departmental funding on the basis of a suite of performance indicators relating to teaching and learning (University of Sydney 2000), and rewards individuals for excellence in teaching.
- Napier University in Scotland (Johnston 2003), whose commitment to improving retention was recorded earlier.

What these institutions have in common is a sustained and principled commitment to student success. The key words here are 'principled' and 'sustained': quick fixes are unlikely to give lasting benefits. How many institutional leaders will be prepared to sow the seeds of a harvest that they may not reap? And how many to nurture seedlings they have not sown?

What students can do

Improving student decision-making regarding programmes

1. *Choose their programme wisely.* This means some serious reflection (perhaps assisted by careers advisory services) on what they want to achieve in life, and not entering higher education 'because that is what is expected', or because of family or school pressure. It also means researching what the programmes of interest are really like, going beyond institutional promotional materials, 'league tables' (rankings of institutions) and the generalized advice of the various 'guides to

universities'. The QAA reports on subject provision, where reasonably current, may be helpful but deal with provision in a broad academic area and may miss the essence of a particular programme. The 'positional good' attached to an institution's reputation needs to be weighed against the potential 'fit' of the programme to the student's needs. A strong commitment to the chosen programme helps greatly in coping with the stresses (academic, social, financial) of undertaking a programme.

2. *Avoid rushing their choice.* Last-minute choices may be ill-advised because of the limited opportunity for researching what institutions are able to offer. The 'Clearing'[112] system in the UK, which swings rapidly into operation following the publication of the A Level results, gives students very little time to make their decisions about programme and institution.

3. *If uncertain, do something else for the time being.* Perhaps take 'time out' of the educational system. Taking up employment, undertaking voluntary work, and gaining a broader perspective on the world through travel are three ways in which potential students can help themselves to identify the kinds of programme that they really want to pursue. All three can give rise to items on a curriculum vitae (resumé) that could be attractive to potential employers. Employment has the additional advantage of offering the chance to build up a financial reserve to help with the costs of studying.

The student experience

4. *Be aware that self-motivation is needed.* In higher education, the expectation is that students will be independent and autonomous learners. The change from the high level of supervision typical of school catches a number of students unawares. The need to work towards assignments throughout a semester may not be appreciated sufficiently soon to avoid a frantic rush to complete a number by the stated deadline. One way of helping students to plan their work is to get them, at an early opportunity, to map out their academic commitments for the semester so that they can see where the pressure is likely to build up. They then have a better chance of scheduling their workload in order to prevent massive peaks.

5. *Appreciate that regurgitating the work of others is not enough.* Whilst giving back to assessors what they gave out as teachers can be sufficient to gain a passing grade, it is insufficient to gain a high grade. The expectation is that students will read more deeply into their subject(s), and offer not the unmodified views of authorities but the fruits of their own intellectual efforts supported by appropriate evidence.[113]

6. *Take note of, and act on, formative assessments.* Many academics take considerable trouble to comment constructively on submitted work. Some

students – perhaps those more committed to 'performance' goals than to learning goals – may merely note the grade (with or without satisfaction) and move on. The opportunity to maximize the learning potential is forfeited in such circumstances.

Failure to cope with the demand of the programme

7. *Be prepared for the possibility of low initial grades.* If students are working to misperceived expectations of how to prepare assignments, then work that they believe is quite good may not match the expectations of the programme. The need is to appreciate quickly where things have gone astray, and to set about redeeming the position. Seeking help is not a sign of weakness, but a positive practical action. Rogers' (2002) observations on 'interim failure' (see earlier) are helpful here. Students need to remember that early performances may not weigh significantly in the overall programme assessment in some higher educational systems, and hence poor initial grades may not prejudice ultimate success.
8. *Use apparent failure as a stimulus to learning.* Dweck (1999) notes that the adoption of learning goals is more likely to profit the individual than the adoption of 'performance' goals, particularly when faced with an apparently poor outcome.

Events that impact on students' lives outside the institution

Even the most risk-averse students may find themselves in situations which necessitate withdrawal from higher education, since some things that impinge on students' lives are impossible to predict, such as accidents and ill-health. However, some problems can be anticipated, and appropriate action taken to minimize their impact.

9. *Prepare to manage finances.* Students who have lived independently will probably have appreciated the need to manage their finances, but this can be a new challenge for those leaving home for the first time. Surveys by British banks find many students who do not have their finances under adequate control. Money can vanish remarkably quickly if not well controlled, and credit cards and overdrafts offer only a temporary respite. There is, after all, an unavoidable connection between what is spent and what has to be paid for.[114]
10. *Find out about the environment in which they will be living.* Some students are relatively unaware of the risks that can inhere in the environment in which they obtain accommodation, and suffer burglaries and personal attacks. The likelihood of unpleasant surprises can be reduced if the

students 'check out' the area in which they will be living, and takes basic precautions to maximize the security of themselves and their property.

11. *Be 'streetwise'.* Students need to be aware that some criminals target students as a 'soft touch'. They need to be alert, and to take sensible precautions such as not being alone late at night and/or in risky areas, not showing that they have possessions worth stealing, and the like.

12. *Avoid placing themselves at risk through their own behaviour.* Excesses such as alcohol and drugs exacerbate the risk of withdrawal not only because of the associated immediate risks in the public arena but also because of the deferred risk to academic work.

What the higher education system can do

Improving student decision-making regarding programmes

1. *Operate a post-qualification entry system.* This was a recommendation of the Education and Employment Select Committee (House of Commons 2001b: para. 90), reflecting a view held by many in the higher education sector. The great majority of young students in the UK apply to enter higher education on the basis of predicted examination grades, and conditional acceptances close down options should these grades turn out differently from those that were expected. Further, students may do more or less well than they expected in the different subjects they have studied, and this might have an influence on their preferred choice of programme. Davies and Elias (2003: 28) give some examples of how the inflexibility of the system has worked to the disadvantage of students (who, it might be argued, could have turned the situation to their advantage by opting to take a 'gap year').

The student experience

2. *Ensure that teaching is valued.* The requirement laid on institutions by the Higher Education Funding Council for England to produce, and act on, institutional learning and teaching strategies has focused attention on learning and teaching in English institutions. Policies for the recognition and reward of teaching have begun to bear fruit in the number of professorships that have been awarded for achievements in which teaching has been prominent. In the University of Sydney, teaching expertise is a *requirement* for promotion.[115] The National Teaching Fellowship Scheme, as has that in Australia (AUTC nd), is giving teaching a prominence that it has previously lacked.

3. *Ensure that policy initiatives do not implicitly discourage institutional attention to the student experience.* This is a broader point than the previous one, in

that whilst policy rhetoric might favour learning and teaching (and the student experience in general), other policy initiatives might distract attention from it. The Research Assessment Exercises (RAE) in the UK have drawn academics' attention to the possibility of obtaining extra institutional funding contingent on research performance, and are widely believed to have distracted attention from the support of student learning.

Failure to cope with the demand of the programme

4. *Use the national or state quality assurance apparatus to check that provision meets threshold levels of acceptability.* Institutions should have in place systems to ensure that students receive an experience that is of reasonable quality. The level of external scrutiny should be appropriate to the institution's record – an institution whose retention/completion rates are good and whose graduates are valued in the outside world probably requires a 'lighter touch' than a new institution or one that is moving into new areas of curricular provision. The student's determination of value for money is established by the market, though 'value' here subsumes both the educational experience itself and the economic 'positional good' that attaches to the qualification gained.

5. *Use an appropriate time-scale for computing completion.* In the US, a datum for institutions is the proportion of a cohort that completes in 1.5 times the expected duration of the programme (Gaither et al. 1994), reflecting the way that many students choose to progress through their studies. Astin and Oseguera (2002) show that, although completion rates continue to rise after six years, the bulk of completions are achieved by that time. The HEFCE (2002) indicators are computed to a tighter time-scale which, as students' participation in the UK edges in form towards that in the US, looks increasingly constrained. The HEFCE methodology may, in addition, implicitly discriminate against institutions whose students come from poorer backgrounds and opt to take longer over their studies as they cope with financial difficulties and other vicissitudes.

6. *Be relatively relaxed about retention and completion.* The more the costs of higher education are borne by the student (and the more they exert more of a consumer-like role as regards participation), the less should be the significance of retention and completion statistics to a national system. In a fully market-driven system, the logic is that retention and completion should not be an issue – save in respect of the national need for appropriate numbers of qualified entrants to the workforce.[116] Where the interest lies in institutional performance, as seen in terms of the success of the student/institutional partnership, the unit of study (rather than the year or the programme) may be the most appropriate unit of analysis (Yorke 1999b: 81ff).

Events that impact on students' lives outside the institution

7. *Ensure that the system of funding for students is as straightforward as possible.* Financial support for students in the UK has been criticized for its complexity (UUK 2002a) which, in the English context, was demonstrated by the National Audit Office (NAO 2002b: 30). If the system of support funding is complex, then students may not take full advantage of the support that is available to them, and reach the point where they decide erroneously that the only feasible course of action is to withdraw.
8. *Ensure that initiatives designed to support designated groups of students are supported by related initiatives.* Disadvantaged students are at greater risk than others, yet policy initiatives designed to encourage them into higher education can be undermined by policy decisions taken elsewhere, simply because the policy connections have not been made. The system of support for students needs to fit policy considerations such as equity, for example. Hu and St John (2001) studied the effect of aid policy in Indiana by looking at the relative persistence rates for different ethnic groups in three discrete academic years (1990–91, 1993–94 and 1996–97). They concluded that the provision of aid did help to increase the persistence of disadvantaged groups and hence helped towards the equalizing of opportunity.

> . . . states or university systems may need to take a more activist role in promoting academic improvements that equalize opportunities. Given that students of color, as well as students with below-C averages, were less likely to persist, remediation may not be an adequate policy. Rather, it is important for educational systems to assess how well they support the learning needs of diverse students and then use this information to develop more workable strategies.
>
> Hu and St John (2001: 283)

Hu and St John point to the need for synergy in policy-making and implementation.

Epilogue

We have shown in this book that concepts such as retention, attrition and student success are complex in a number of respects – definitionally, theoretically, causally and empirically. Whilst there is often a desire to strip things down, to make them clear-cut and neatly linear in terms of cause and effect, our postmodernist experience tells us that we have to work with complexity and non-linearity as we grapple with the challenge of trying to help our students to become successful.

Solutions to problems in the field of human behaviour are rarely simple. The literature bears witness to the difficulty of understanding why one student withdraws from higher education whereas another, with apparently similar background and characteristics, perseveres and succeeds. It also suggests that we need to judge student success in terms of a wider range of criteria than sometimes is adopted – whilst academic achievement is to be valued, there are forms of achievement which are in different respects valuable to society (though these are more difficult to index and may not figure prominently in current assessment practices). It is doubtful whether existing performance indicator systems have the sensitivity to capture all that is worthy in student achievement.

When we stand back from the individual student, we can appreciate that certain circumstances are likely to encourage student success (however defined) and others to discourage it. A major concern in this book has been how institutions can increase the probability of student success – actions such as creating a sense of belonging, employing pedagogic practices that promote engagement, adopting approaches to assessment that enhance learning (especially during the period when students are coming to terms with the demands of higher education), and providing accessible and helpful support services. Institutions cannot guarantee students' success, since a great deal depends on students' own commitment and determination, but they can, through the ways in which they go about their work, 'bend the odds' in favour of success – or of withdrawal.

When we stand back even further, we can see the similarities and differences between higher education systems. All exhibit, to varying extents, human capital and social justice as philosophical substrates in their concerns to see opportunities opened up to those who can benefit, irrespective of their origins. All want to maximize the level of student success, with economic prosperity as the driver. In all, student funding is an issue. However, in different systems the magnitude of the challenges varies. Bunting's exposition (Chapter 2) shows that achieving student success in South Africa is a far greater challenge, in terms of both social justice and human capital, than it is in the richer countries.

The suggestions we made in Chapter 10 have broad applicability in higher education, though some are likely to need some adjustment to suit particular national systems. Their applicability stems from a grounding in theory, empirical findings and practical experience. They also reflect our belief that, as educators and administrators, we have to act with intelligence in the ways in which we design our educational provision, and in the ways in which we respond to our students' needs. There are rarely 'quick fixes', which imply a relatively straightforward causality. Much more often, the situations require us to act with informed professional judgement. We hope that this book will help to enhance the professionalism that students are entitled to expect.

References

Abramson, M. and Jones, P. (2003) Final report of the GNVQ Flying Start Bridging Project, 1999–2001: Improving student retention at the University of Central Lancashire. Mimeo, University of Central Lancashire, Preston.

Anderson, D. S. and Vervoom, A. E. (1983) *Access to Privilege: Patterns of Participation in Australian Postsecondary Education.* Canberra: ANU Press.

Anderson, J. A. and Adams, A. M. (1992) Acknowledging the learning styles of diverse student populations: Implications for instructional design, in N. V. N. Chism (ed.) *Teaching for Diversity*, Vol. 49. San Francisco, CA: Jossey Bass.

Archer, L. and Hutchings, M. (2000) Bettering yourself? Discourses of risk, cost and benefit in the young working class non-participants' construction of higher education, *British Journal of Sociology of Education*, 21(4): 555–75.

Archer, L., Hutchings, M. and Ross, A. (2003) *Higher Education and Social Class: Issues of Exclusion and Inclusion.* London: RoutledgeFalmer.

Astin, A. W. (1984) Student involvement: A developmental theory for higher education, *Journal of College Student Personnel*, 25(2): 297–308.

Astin, A. W. (1991) *Assessment for Excellence.* New York: American Council on Education and Macmillan.

Astin, A. W. (1993) *What Matters in College? Four Critical Years Revisited.* San Francisco, CA: Jossey-Bass.

Astin, A. W. and Oseguera, L. (2002) *Degree Attainment Rates at American Colleges and Universities.* Los Angeles, CA: Higher Education Research Institute, University of California.

Astin, A. W., Tsui, L. and Avalos, J. (1996) *Degree Attainment Rates at American Colleges and Universities: Effects of Race, Gender and Institutional Type.* Los Angeles, CA: Higher Education Research Institute, University of California.

Aungles, P., Karmel, T. and Wu, T. (2000) *Demographic and Social Change: Implications for Education Funding. Department of Education, Training and Youth Affairs*, Canberra. www.detya.gov.au/archive/highered/occpaper/00B/default.htm (accessed on 20 July 2003).

Ausubel, D. P. (1968) *Educational Psychology: A Cognitive View.* London: Holt, Rinehart and Winston.

AUTC (nd) *Australian Awards for University Teaching.* www.autc.gov.au/aw/aw.htm (accessed 8 July 2003).

Bakan, D. (1967) *On Method: Towards a Reconstruction of Psychological Investigation*. San Francisco, CA: Jossey-Bass.

Baker, K. (1989) Higher education – the next 25 years. Speech presented at University of Lancaster, 17 January.

Bandura, A. (1997) *Self-efficacy: The Exercise of Control*. New York: Freeman.

Banta, T. (1988) Assessment as an instrument of state funding policy, in T. Banta (ed.) *Implementing Outcomes Assessment: Promise and Perils [New Directions for Institutional Research No.59]*, pp. 81–94. San Francisco, CA: Jossey-Bass.

Barberet, R., Fisher, B. S., Farrell, G. and Taylor, H. (2003) University student safety: Findings 194. www.homeoffice.gov.uk/rds/pdfs2/r194.pdf (accessed on 20 July 2003).

Barke, M., Braidford, P., Houston, M., Hunt, A., Lincoln, I., Morphet, C., Stone, I. and Walker, A. (2000) *Students in the Labour Market: Nature, Extent and Implications of Term-time Employment among University of Northumbria Undergraduates [Research Report 215]*. London: Department for Education and Skills.

Baty, P. (2003) Just 10 students may blight careers, *The Times Higher Education Supplement*, No.1595, 27 June.

Bean, J. P. and Eaton, S. B. (2000) A psychological model of college student retention, in J. M. Braxton (ed.) *Reworking the Departure Puzzle*, pp. 48–61. Nashville: Vanderbilt University Press.

Bean, J. P. and Metzner, B. S. (1985) A conceptual model of non-traditional student attrition, *Review of Educational Research*, 55(4): 485–540.

Becker, G. S. (1975) *Human Capital*. Chicago: Chicago University Press.

Berger, J. B. (1997) Students' sense of community in residence halls, social integration, and first-year persistence, *Journal of College Student Development*, 38(5): 441–52.

Berger, J. B. (2000) Optimizing Capital, Social Reproduction, and Undergraduate Persistence, in J. M. Braxton (ed.) *Reworking the Student Departure Puzzle*, pp. 95–124. Nashville: Vanderbilt University Press.

Berger, J. B. (2001–2002) Understanding the organisational nature of student persistence: empirically based recommendations for practice, *Journal of College Student Retention*, 3(1): 3–21.

Berger, J. B. and Braxton, J. M. (1998) Revising Tinto's Interactionalist Theory of Student Departure through theory elaboration: Examining the role of organizational attributes in the persistence process, *Research in Higher Education*, 39(2): 103–19.

Berger, J. B. and Milem, J. F. (1999) The role of student involvement and perceptions of integration in a causal model of student persistence, *Research in Higher Education*, 40(6): 641–64.

Biggs, J. (2003) *Teaching for Quality Learning at University*, 2nd edn. Maidenhead: Society for Research in Higher Education and Open University Press.

Black, P. and Wiliam, D. (1998) Assessment and classroom learning, *Assessment in Education*, 5(1): 7–74.

Blair, T. (2001) *Prime Minister's Speech to 2001 Labour Party Conference*. www.politics.guardian.co.uk/labour2001/story/0,1414,562007,00.html (accessed on 20 July 2003).

Blundell, R., Dearden, L., Goodman, A. and Reed, H. (1997) *Higher Education, Employment and Earnings in Britain*. London: Institute of Fiscal Studies.

Blunden, R. (2002) *First Year Student Persistence and Performance and the Nexus with ENTER Scores (subsequent to the first census date 2001) across eight subjects at La Trobe*

University. Melbourne: La Trobe University Academic Development Unit.

Blunkett, D. (2000) Higher Education Funding for 2001–02 and Beyond. Letter received by Sir Michael Checkland, Chair of Higher Education Funding Council for England, 29 November.

Borden, V. and Evenbeck, S. (2003) Developing principles for undergraduate learning that align primary, secondary and tertiary education with each other and with workforce requirements. Paper presented to the EAIR-AIR Joint Seminar on Workforce Development and Higher Education, Amsterdam, 12–14 June.

Borland, K. W. (2001–2002) Assessing retention: six steps and four paradigms, *Journal of College Student Retention*, 3(4): 365–79.

Boud, D. (1995) Assessment and learning: contradictory or complementary?, in P. Knight (ed.) *Assessment for Learning in Higher Education*, pp. 35–48. London: Kogan Page.

Bourdieu, P. (1973) Cultural reproduction and social reproduction, in R. Brown (ed.) *Knowledge, Education and Cultural Change*, pp. 487–510. London: Tavistock.

Bourdieu, P. and Passeron, J. C. (1977) *Reproduction in Education, Society and Culture*. London: Sage.

Bourner, T., Reynolds, A., Hamed, M. and Barnett, R. (1991) *Part-time Students and their Experience of Higher Education*. Buckingham: SRHE and Open University Press.

Bowden, R. (2000) Fantasy higher education: university and college league tables, *Quality in Higher Education*, 6(1): 41–60.

Braxton, J. and McClendon, S. A. (2001–2002) The fostering of social integration and retention through institutional practice, *Journal of College Student Retention: Research, Theory and Practice*, 3(1): 57–71.

Braxton, J. M. (2000a) Reinvigorating Theory and Research on the Departure Puzzle, in J. M. Braxton (ed.) *Reworking the Student Departure Puzzle*, pp. 257–74. Nashville: Vanderbilt University Press.

Braxton, J. M. (2000b) Reworking the Student Departure Puzzle, in J. M. Braxton (ed.) *Reworking the Student Departure Puzzle*, pp. 1–8. Nashville: Vanderbilt University Press.

Braxton, J. M., Bray, N. J. and Berger, J. B. (2000) Faculty teaching skills and their influence on the college student departure process, *Journal of College Student Development*, 41: 215–27.

Braxton, J. M. and Brier, E. M. (1998) Melding organizational and interactional theories of student attrition: A path analytic study, *Review of Higher Education*, 13(1): 47–61.

Braxton, J. M. and Lien, L. A. (2000) The viability of academic integration as a central construct in Tinto's interactionalist theory of student departure, in J. M. Braxton (ed.) *Reworking the Student Departure Puzzle*, pp. 11–28. Nashville: Vanderbilt University Press.

Braxton, J. M., Milem, J. F. and Sullivan, A. S. (2000) The influence of active learning on the college student departure process: Toward a revision of Tinto's theory, *Journal of Higher Education*, 71(5): 569–90.

Braxton, J. M. and Mundy, M. E. (2001) Powerful institutional levers to reduce college student departure, *Journal of College Student Retention: Research, Theory and Practice*, 3(1): 91–118.

Braxton, J. M., Sullivan, A. V. and Johnson, R. M. (1997) Appraising Tinto's theory of college student departure, in J. Smart (ed.) *Higher Education: Handbook of Theory and Research*, Vol. 12, pp. 107–64. New York: Agathon.

Braxton, J. M., Vesper, N. and Hossler, D. (1995) Expectations for college and student persistence, *Research in Higher Education*, 36: 595–612.

Brown, G. (1995) *Stopping Distance: Factors in the Discontinuation of Off-Campus Students at Deakin University.* Toorak: School of Social Inquiry, Deakin University.

Bunting, I. A. (1994) *A Legacy of Inequality.* Cape Town: University of Cape Town Press.

Bunting, I. A. (2001a) *Data Produced for the National Working Group on the Restructuring of the Higher Education Landscape.* Pretoria: Department of Education.

Bunting, I. A. (2001b) *Higher Education Graduation Rates: Benchmarks in the National Plan for Higher Education.* Pretoria: Department of National Education.

Bunting, I. A. (2002a) Funding, in N. Cloete (ed.) *Transformation in Higher Education: Global Pressures and Local Realities in South Africa*, pp. 115–146. Cape Town: Juta Press.

Bunting, I. A. (2002b) The higher education landscape under apartheid, in N. Cloete (ed.) *Transformation in Higher Education: Global Pressures and Local Realities in South Africa*, pp. 58–86. Cape Town: Juta Press.

Bunting, I. A. (2002c) Student inflow and outflow, in P. Pillay and N. Cloete (eds) *Strategic Co-operation Scenarios: Post-school Education in the Eastern Cape.*, pp. 56–68. Pretoria: Centre for Higher Education Transformation.

Cabrera, A. F., Castaneda, M. B., Nora, A. and Hengstler, D. (1992) The convergence between two theories of college persistence, *Journal of Higher Education*, 63(2): 143–64.

Cabrera, A. F., Nora, A., Terenzini, P. T., Pascarella, E. and Hagedorn, L. S. (1999) Campus racial climate and the adjustment of students to college: A comparison between White students and African-American students, *Journal of Higher Education*, 70(2): 134–60.

Callender, C. (2003) *Attitudes to Debt: School Leavers' and Further Education Students' Attitudes to Debt and their Impact on Participation in Higher Education.* London: Universities UK.

Callender, C. and Kemp, M. (2000) *Changing Student Finances: Income, Expenditure and Take-up of Student Loans among Full time and Part Time Higher Education Students in 1998/9. [Research Report RR213].* London: Department for Education and Employment.

Cave, M., Hanney, S., Henkel, M. and Kogan, M. (1997) *The Use of Performance Indicators in Higher Education: the Challenge of the Quality Movement.* London: Jessica Kingsley.

CDP (1987) Performance indicators: a position statement. Mimeo, Committee of Directors of Polytechnics, London.

Chickering, A. W. and Gamson, Z. F. (1987) Seven principles for good practice in undergraduate education, *AAHE Bulletin*, 39(7): 3–7.

Choy, S. P. (2002) *Access and Persistence: Fndings from 10 years of Longitudinal Research on Students.* Washington DC: American Council on Education.

Claxton, G. (1998) *Hare Brain, Tortoise Mind.* London: Fourth Estate.

CNAA/PCFC (1990) *The Measurement of Value-added in Higher Education.* London: Council for National Academic Awards and Polytechnics and Colleges Funding Council.

Cohen, P. (1989) Student ratings of instruction and student achievement: A meta-analysis of multisection validity studies, *Review of Educational Research*, 51: 281–309.

Committee on Higher Education (1963) *Higher Education: Report of the Committee Appointed by the Prime Minister under the Chairmanship of Lord Robbins 1961–1963*, Cm 2154. London: HMSO.

CVCP (1985) *Report of the Steering Committee for Efficiency Studies in Universities [The Jarratt Report]*. London: Committee of Vice Chancellors and Principals.

CVCP (1994) *University Management Statistics and Performance Indicators in the UK*. London: Committee of Vice Chancellors and Principals.

CVCP/UGC (1986) *Performance indicators in universities: A First Statement by a Joint CVCP/UGC Working Group*. London: Committee of Vice Chancellors and Principals.

Davies, R. and Elias, P. (2003) *Dropping Out: A Study of Early Leavers from Higher Education*. London: Department for Education and Skills.

DEET (1990) *A Fair Chance for All: National and Institutional Planning for Equity in Higher Education, a Discussion Paper*. Canberra: AGPS.

Department of Education (1982) *An Investigation of Government Funding of Universities*. Pretoria: Department of Education.

Department of Education (1997) *A Programme for the Transformation of Higher Education*, White Paper 3. Pretoria: Department of Education and Science.

Department of Education (2001a) *National Plan for Higher Education*. Pretoria: Department of Education.

Department of Education (2001b) *Report of the National Working Group to the Minister of Education*. Pretoria: Department of Education.

Department of Education (2001c) *Student Statistics Tables (1999–2001)*. Pretoria: Higher Education Management Information System.

Department of Education (2002a) *Funding of Public Higher Education: A New Framework*. Pretoria: Department of Education.

Department of Education (2002b) *Information on the State Budget for Higher Education*. Pretoria: Department of Education.

Department of Education (2002c) *A New Institutional Landscape for Higher Education*. Pretoria: Department of Education.

DEST (2001) *Characteristics and Performance Indicators of Australian Higher Education Institutions*. Occasional Paper Series 01-B. Canberra: Higher Education Division, Department of Education, Science and Training.

DEST (2002a) *Higher Education Report for the 2002–2004 Triennium*. Canberra: Australian Government Publishing Service.

DEST (2002b) *Students 2001: Selected Higher Education Statistics*. Canberra: Australian Government Publishing Service.

DEST (2003) *The Higher Education Sector in Australia*. www.detya.gov.au/highered/unis.htm. Canberra: Australian Government Publishing Service (accessed on 20 July 2003).

DETYA (1999) *Equity in Higher Education*. Occasional Paper 99A. Canberra: Higher Education Division.

DETYA (2000) *Characteristics and Performance Indicators of Higher Education Institutions, 2000: Preliminary Report*. www.detya.gov.au/archive/highered/statistics/characteristics/contents.htm (accessed on 5 April 2001).

Dewey, J. (1916) *Essays in Experimental Logic*. New York: Dover.

DfES (2003a) *The Future of Higher Education*. London: HMSO.

DfES (2003b) *Student Funding: Findings from a Two-stage Programme of Qualitative Research on the Funding of Higher Education*. London: Department for Education and Skills.

Dobson, I. (2001) How has massification changed the shape of Australian universities?, *Tertiary Education and Management*, 7(4): 295–310.

Dobson, I. and Sharma, R. (1993) Student Progress: A Study of the Experience in

Victorian Tertiary Institutions, *Journal of Tertiary Education Administration*, 15(2): 203–11.

Dobson, I., Sharma, R. and Haydon, A. (1996) *Evaluation of the Relative Performance of Commencing Undergraduate Students in Australian Universities*. Adelaide: Australian Credit Transfer Agency.

Dochy, F. J. R. C., Segers, M. S. R. and Wijnen, W. H. F. W. (eds) (1990) *Management Information and Performance Indicators in Higher Education: An International Issue*. Assen/Maastricht: van Gorcum.

Durkheim, E. (1951) *Suicide: A Study in Sociology*. Glencoe, Illinois: Free Press.

Dweck, C. S. (1999) *Self-theories: Their Role in Motivation, Personality and Development*. Philadelphia, PA: Psychology Press.

Eaton, S. B. and Bean, J. P. (1995) An approach/avoidance behavioral model of college student attrition, *Research in Higher Education*, 36(6): 617–45.

Eckel, P. (2001) A world apart? Higher education transformation in the US and South Africa, *Higher Education Policy*, 14(2): 103–15.

Eliot, T. S. (1962) *Collected Plays*. London: Faber.

Ewell, P. (1993) Developing statewide performance indicators for higher education: policy themes and variations. Mimeo, NCHEMS, Boulder, CO.

Ewell, P. T. (1999) Linking performance measures to resource allocation: exploring unmapped terrain, *Quality in Higher Education*, 5(3): 191–209.

Ewell, P. T. and Jones, D. P. (1994) Pointing the way: indicators as policy tools in higher education, in S. Ruppert (ed.) *Charting Higher Education Accountability: A Sourcebook on State-level Performance Indicators*, pp. 6–16. Denver, CO: Education Commission of the States.

Feldman, K. (1998) The association between student ratings of specific instructional dimensions and student achievement: Refining and extending the synthesis data from multisection validity studies, *Research in Higher Education*, 30(6): 583–645.

Finifter, D. H., Baldwin, R. G. and Thelin, J. R. (1991) *The Uneasy Public Policy Triangle: Quality, Diversity, and Budgetary Efficiency*. New York: ACE-Macmillan.

Forsyth, A. and Furlong, A. (2003) *Losing Out? Socioeconomic Disadvantage and Experience in Further and Higher Education*. Bristol: The Policy Press.

Foster, J., Houston, M., Knox, H. and Rimmer, R. (2002) *Surviving First Year: Access, Retention and Value Added*, Report on the 2000–2001 Pilot. Paisley: University of Paisley.

Gadamer, H.-G. (1975) *Truth and Method*, 2nd edn. London: Sheed and Ward.

Gaither, G., Nedwek, B. and Neal, J. E. (1994) *Measuring Up: The Promises and Pitfalls of Performance Indicators in Higher Education*, ASHE Report no. 5. Washington, DC: George Washington University.

Gamage, D. T. and Mininberg, E. (2003) Australian and American higher education: Key issues of the first decade of the 21st century, *Higher Education*, 45(2): 183–202.

Gloria, A. M. and Robinson Kurpius, S. (2001) Influences of self-beliefs, social support and comfort in the university environment on the academic non-persistence decisions of American Indian undergraduates, *Cultural Diversity and Ethnic Minority Psychology*, 7(1): 88–102.

Goleman, D. (1996) *Emotional Intelligence: Why It Can Matter More Than IQ*. London: Bloomsbury.

Grenfell, M. and James, D. (1998) *Bourdieu and Education: Acts of Practical Theory*. London: Falmer Press.

Grierson, J. and Parr, P. (1994) *I Only Left Because ...: An Investigation into the Reasons for Student Withdrawal from the University of Western Sydney.* Macarthur: Student Services Division, UWS.

Harvey, O. J., Hunt, D. E. and Schroder, H. M. (1961) *Conceptual Systems and Personality Organization.* New York: Wiley.

HEFCE (1999a) *Performance Indicators in Higher Education in the UK 1996–97, 1997–98.* Bristol: Higher Education Funding Council for England.

HEFCE (1999b) *Performance Indicators in Higher Education: First Report of the Performance Indicators Steering Group.* Bristol: Higher Education Funding Council for England.

HEFCE (2000) *Performance Indicators in Higher Education in the UK 1997–98, 1998–99.* Bristol: Higher Education Funding Council for England.

HEFCE (2001a) *Performance Indicators in Higher Education in the UK 1998–99, 1999–2000.* Bristol: Higher Education Funding Council for England.

HEFCE (2001b) *Strategies for Widening Participation in Higher Education.* Bristol: Higher Education Funding Council for England.

HEFCE (2001c) *Strategies for Widening Participation in Higher Education: A Guide to Good Practice*, Report 01/36. Bristol: Higher Education Funding Council for England.

HEFCE (2002) *Performance Indicators in Higher Education in the UK, 1999–2000, 2000–1.* Bristol: Higher Education Funding Council for England.

Helland, P. A., Stallings, H. J. and Braxton, J. M. (2001–2002) The fulfillment of expectations for college and student departure decisions, *Journal of College Student Retention*, 3(4): 381–96.

HESA (2002) *Students in Higher Education Institutions 2000/01.* Cheltenham: Higher Education Statistics Agency.

House of Commons (1999) Early Years and Higher Education. Forthcoming inquiries by the Education and Employment Sub-Committee, 28 October. At http://www.parliament.uk/commons/selcom89/edepnt41.htm (accessed on 7 December 2003).

House of Commons (2000) Student retention call for evidence. Education and Employment Select Committee on Higher Education, 21 December. At http://www.parliament.uk/commons/selcom/edepnt03.htm (accessed on 7 December 2003).

House of Commons (2001a) Government's response to the Fourth Report from the Committee Session 2000–01: Higher Education: Access, 28 March. London, published by Authority of the House of Commons.

House of Commons (2001b) *Higher Education: Access.* Report, together with the proceedings of the Committee, Minutes of Evidence taken before the Education Sub-committee and Appendices to the Minutes of Evidence. London: The Stationery Office.

House of Commons (2001c) *Higher Education: Student retention.* Report, together with the proceedings of the Committee, Minutes of Evidence taken before the Education Sub-committee and Appendices to the Minutes of Evidence, 13 March. London: The Stationery Office.

House of Commons (2001d) Sixth Special Report on Access responses from the Government, 8 November. London, published by Authority of the House of Commons.

House of Commons (2002) *Post-16 Student Support.* Hansard. www.publications.parliament.uk/pa/cm200102/cmselect/cmeduski/445/44502.htm (accessed on 20 July 2003).

House of Commons (2003) *The Future of Higher Education: Fifth Report of Session 2002–03 – Volume 1*. London: HMSO.

Hu, S. and St John, E. P. (2001) Student persistence in a public higher education system: understanding racial and ethnic differences, *Journal of Higher Education*, 72(3): 265–86.

Hurtado, S. and Carter, D. F. (1997) Effects of college transition and perceptions of the campus racial climate on Latino students' sense of belonging, *Sociology of Education*, 70(4): 324–45.

Institute for Scientific Information (2002) *Web of Knowledge*. www.isinet.com (accessed on 20 July 2003).

James, R. (2000) *TAFE, University or Work? The Early Preferences and Choices of Students in Years 10, 11 and 12*. Adelaide: National Council for Vocational Education Research.

James, R. (2002) *Socio-Economic Background and Higher Education Participation: An Analysis of School Students' Aspirations and Expectations*. Canberra: AGPS.

James, R., Wyn, J., Baldwin, G., Hepworth, G., McInnis, C. and Stephanou, A. (1999) *Rural and Isolated School Students and their Higher Education Choices*. Canberra: AGPS.

Johnes, J. and Taylor, J. (1990) *Performance Indicators in Higher Education*. Buckingham: SRHE and Open University Press.

Johnes, J. and Taylor, J. (1991) Non-completion of a degree course and its effect on the subsequent experience of non-completers in the labour market, *Studies in Higher Education*, 16(1): 73–81.

Johnson, D. W., Johnson, R. T. and Smith, K. A. (1991) *Cooperative Learning: Increasing College Faculty Instructional Productivity*. Washington, DC: Graduate School of Education and Human Development, George Washington University.

Johnston, V. (2003) Mission Impossible?, in H. Edwards, D. Baume and G. Webb (eds) *Staff and Educational Development – Case Studies, Experience and Practice*, pp. 114–124. London: Kogan Page.

JPIWG (1994a) Consultative Report. Mimeo, Higher Education Funding Council for England, Bristol.

JPIWG (1994b) Explanatory and statistical material to accompany Consultative Report. Mimeo, Higher Education Funding Council for England, Bristol.

Kells, H. R. (1990) *The Development of Performance Indicators for Higher Education: A Compendium for Eleven Countries*. Paris: OECD.

Kells, H. R. (1993) *The Development of Performance Indicators for Higher Education: A Compendium for Twelve Countries*. Paris: OECD.

Keohane, N. O. (1999) The American Campus, in D. Smith and A. K. Langslow (eds) *The Idea of a University*, pp. 48–67. London: Jessica Kingsley.

Knight, P. T. (2002) *Being a Teacher in Higher Education*. Buckingham: SRHE and Open University Press.

Knight, P. T. and Yorke, M. (2003) *Assessment, Learning and Employability*. Maidenhead: SRHE and Open University Press.

Knight, P. T. and Yorke, M. (2004) *Learning, Curriculum and Employability in Higher Education*. London: RoutledgeFalmer.

Krakower, J. (1985) *Assessing Organizational Effectiveness: Considerations and Procedures*. Boulder, CO: NCHEMS.

Krause, K., McInnis, C. and Welle, C. (2002) Student engagement: The role of peers in undergraduate student experience. Paper presented to the Society for Research into Higher Education Conference, Glasgow, UK, 10–12 December.

Kuh, G. D. (2001–2002) Organizational culture and student persistence: Prospects and puzzles, *Journal of College Student Retention*, 3(1): 23–39.

Kuh, G. D. (nd) The National Survey of Student Engagement: conceptual framework and overviews of psychometric properties. www.iub.edu/~nsse/html/psychometric_framework_2002.htm (accessed on 19 July 2003).

Kuh, G. D. and Love, P. G. (2000) A cultural perspective on student departure, in J. M. Braxton (ed.) *Reworking the Student Departure Puzzle: New Theory and Research on College Student Retention*, pp. 196–212. Nashville: Vanderbilt University Press.

Kuh, G. D. and Whitt, E. J. (1988) *The Invisible Tapestry: Culture in American Colleges and Universities*. Washington, DC: Association for the Study of Higher Education.

Layer, G., Srivastava, A., Thomas, L. and Yorke, M. (2002) Student Success: Building for Change, in Action on Access (2003) *Student Success in Higher Education*, pp. 73–136. Bradford: University of Bradford.

Liljander, J.-P. (1998) Gains and losses on academic transfer market: dropping out and course-switching in higher education, *British Journal of Sociology of Education*, 19(4): 479–95.

Linke, R. (1991) *Performance Indicators in Higher Education*. Canberra: Australian Government Publishing Service.

Long, M. (1994) *A Study of the Academic Results of On-Campus and off-Campus Students: Comparative Performance Within Four Australian Tertiary Institutions*. Canberra: AGPS.

Long, M. and Hayden, M. (2001) *Paying their Way: A Survey of Australian Undergraduate University Student Finances, 2000*. www.avcc.edu.au/news/public_statements/publications/final_report_rev_22_oct_01.pdf (accessed on 20 July 2003).

Longden, B. (2000) Elitism to inclusion – some developmental tensions, *Educational Studies*, 26(4): 454–74.

Longden, B. (2001a) Funding policy in higher education – contested terrain, *Research Papers in Education*, 16(2): 1–22.

Longden, B. (2001b) *Leaving College Early: A Qualitative Case Study*. www.hope.ac.uk/staff/longden (accessed on 28 July 2003).

Longden, B. (2002a) Echoing policy in the student experience of leaving college early. Paper presented at the European Association of Institutional Research Forum Conference, Prague.

Longden, B. (2002b) Retention rates – renewed interest but whose interest is being served?, *Research Papers in Education*, 17(1): 3–30.

Love, B. J. (1993) Issues and problems in the retention of Black students in predominantly White institutions of higher education. *Equity and Excellence in Education*, 26(1): 27–36.

Love, P. G. (1995) Exploring the impact of student affairs professionals on student outcomes, *Journal of College Student Development*, 36(2): 162–70.

Martin, Y. M., Maclachlan, M. and Karmel, T. (2001) *Undergraduate Completion Rates: An Update*. www.detya.gov.au/highered/occpaper/01f/default.htm (Canberra, Department of Education, Science and Training – accessed on 20 July 2003).

Marton, F. and Säljö, R. (1976) On qualitative differences in learning. I – Outcome and process, *British Journal of Educational Psychology*, 46(1): 4–11.

Marzano, R. J. (1998) *A Theory-based Meta-analysis of Research on Instruction*. Aurora, CO: Mid-continent Regional Educational Laboratory.

McDonough, P. (1994) Buying and selling higher education: The social construction of the college applicant, *Journal of Higher Education*, 65(4): 427–46.

McDonough, P. (1997) *Choosing Colleges: How Social Class and Schools Structure Opportunity.* Albany: State University of New York.

McGivney, V. (1996) *Staying or Leaving the Course: Non-completion and Retention of Mature Students in Further and Higher Education.* Leicester: National Institute of Adult Continuing Education.

McGuire, M. D. (1995) Validity issues for reputational studies, in R. D. Walleri and M. K. Moss (eds) *Evaluating and Responding to College Guidebooks and Rankings,* New Directions for Institutional Research No. 88, pp. 45–59, San Francisco, CA: Jossey-Bass.

McInnis, C. (2001) Researching the first year experience: where to from here?, *Higher Education Research and Development,* 20(2): 105–114.

McInnis, C. and Hartley, R. (2002) *Managing Study and Work.* Canberra: Department of Education, Science and Training.

McInnis, C., Hartley, R., Polesel, J. and Teese, R. (2000a) *Non-Completion in Vocational Education and Training and Higher Education: A Literature Review Commissioned by the Department of Education, Training and Youth Affairs.* Canberra: Department of Education, Training and Youth Affairs.

McInnis, C. and James, R. (1995) *First Year on Campus: Diversity in the Initial Experiences of Australian Undergraduates.* Canberra: AGPS.

McInnis, C., James, R. and Hartley, R. (2000) *Trends in the First Year Experience in Australian Universities.* Canberra: AGPS.

McMillan, D. W. and Chavis, D. M. (1986) Sense of community: A definition and theory, *Journal of Community Psychology,* 14(1): 6–23.

Mentkowski, M. et al. (2000) *Learning that Lasts: Integrating Learning Development and Performance in College and Beyond.* San Francisco, CA: Jossey-Bass.

Metzner, B. S. and Bean, J. P. (1987) The estimation of a conceptual model of non-traditional undergraduate student attrition, *Research in Higher Education,* 27(1): 15–38.

Milem, J. F. and Berger, J. B. (1997) A modified model of college student persistence: Exploring the relationship between Astin's theory of involvement and Tinto's theory of student departure, *Journal of College Student Development,* 38(4): 387–400.

Ministry of Education (2002) *Tertiary Education Strategy, 2002/07.* Wellington, New Zealand: Ministry of Education.

Moortgat, J. (1996) *A Study of Dropout in European Higher Education: Case Studies of Five Countries.* Strasbourg: Council of Europe.

Morgan, M., Flanagan, R. and Kellaghan, T. (2001) *A Study of Non-Completion in Undergraduate University Courses.* Dublin: Higher Education Authority.

Morris, E. (2001) First major speech by the Secretary of State for Education and Skills. Speech presented at London Guildhall University, 22 October.

Morrison, H. G., Magennis, S. P. and Carey, L. J. (1995) Performance indicators and league tables: a call for standards, *Higher Education Quarterly,* 49(2): 128–45.

NAB Good Management Practice Group (1987) *Management for a purpose.* London: National Advisory Body for Public Sector Education.

NAO (2002a) *Improving Student Achievement in English Higher Education.* London: National Audit Office.

NAO (2002b) *Widening Participation in Higher Education in England.* London: National Audit Office.

National Commission on Higher Education (1996) *A Framework for Transformation.* Pretoria: National Commission on Higher Education.

Naylor, R. and Smith, J. (2002) *Schooling Effects on Subsequent University Performance: Evidence for the UK University Population*, Warwick Economic Research Papers No. 657. Coventry: Department of Economics, Warwick University.

NCIHE (1997) *Higher Education in the Learning Society, Report of the National Committee of Inquiry.* Norwich: HMSO.

Nelson, B. (2002) *Higher Education at the Crossroads: An overview paper.* www.dest. gov.au/crossroads/pubs.htm (Department of Education, Science and Training – accessed on 20 July 2003).

Nelson, B. (2003) *Higher Education Report for 2003 to 2005 Triennium.* www.detya. gov.au/highered/he_report/2003_2005/default.htm (accessed on 20 July 2003).

Newcomb, T. M. (1966) The general nature of peer group influence, in T. M. Wilson and E. K. Wilson (eds) *College Peer Groups: Problems and Prospects for Research*, pp. 2–16. Chicago: Aldine.

Nora, A. (2001–2002) The depiction of significant others in Tinto's 'Rites of Passage': A reconceptualisation of the influences of family and community in the persistence process, *Journal of College Student Retention*, 3(1): 41–56.

Nora, A., and Cabrera, A. F. (1996) The role of perceptions in prejudice and discrimination and the adjustment of minority students to college, *Journal of Higher Education*, 67(2): 119–48.

Nora, A., Attinasi, L. C. and Matonak, A. (1990) Testing qualitative indicators of pre-college factors in Tinto's attrition model: A community college perspective, *The Review of Higher Education*, 13(3): 337–56.

OECD (2000) *Education at a Glance: OECD Indicators – Education & Skills.* Paris: OECD.

OECD (2002) *Education at a Glance: OECD Indicators – Education & Skills.* Paris: OECD.

Office of Institutional Research – BGSU (2001) *An Analytic Study of First Year Student Retention at BGSU.* www.bgsu.edu/offices/ir/studies/FreshmanRetention/retention.html (accessed on 20 July 2003).

Pascarella, E. and Terenzini, P. (1991) *How College Affects Students: Findings and Insights from Twenty Years of Research.* San Francisco: Jossey-Bass Inc.

Pascarella, E. T., Edison, M., Nora, A., Hagedorn, L. and Braxton, J. M. (1996) Effects of teacher organization/preparation and teacher skill/clarity on general cognitive skills in college, *Journal of College Student Development*, 37(1): 2–19.

Pascarella, E. T., Terenzini, P. T. and Wolfle, L. M. (1986) Orientation to college and freshman year persistence/withdrawal decisions, *Journal of Higher Education*, 57(2): 155–75.

Pedhazur, E. J. (1997) *Multiple Regression in Behavioral Research: Explanation and Prediction*, 3rd edn. Fort Worth: Harcourt Brace.

Pelling, N. (2001) A new approach to non-traditional student recruitment and retention, *Australian Universities Review*, 44(1/2): 18–20.

Pintrich, P. R. (2000) The role of goal orientation in self-regulated learning, in M. Boekaerts, P. Pintrich and M. Zeidner (eds) *Handbook of Self-regulation*, pp. 451–502. New York: Academic Press.

Pintrich, P. R. and Schunk, D. H. (1996) *Motivation in Education.* Englewood Cliffs: Prentice-Hall.

Postle, G. D., Clarke, J. R., Skuja, E., Bull, D. D., Batorowicz, K. and McCann, H. A. (1995) Towards excellence in diversity: Educational equity, in G. D. Postle, J. R. Clarke, E. Skuja, D. D. Bull, K. Batorowicz and H. A. McCann (eds) *Australian Higher Education Sector in 1995: Status, Trends and Future Directions.* Toowoomba: USQ Press.

Prosser, M. and Trigwell, K. (1999) *Understanding Learning and Teaching: The Experience in Higher Education.* Buckingham: SRHE and Open University Press.

Ramsay, E., Tranter, D., Sumner, R. and Barrett, S. (1996) *Outcomes of a University's Flexible Admissions and Policies.* Canberra: Program Higher Education Division, DEETYA, Evaluations and Investigations.

Ramsden, P. (1991) A performance indicator of teaching quality in higher education: the Course Experience Questionnaire, *Studies in Higher Education,* 16(2): 129–50.

Read, B., Archer, L. and Leathwood, C. (2003) Challenging cultures? Student conceptions of 'belonging' and 'isolation' at a post-1992 university, *Studies in Higher Education,* 28(3): 261–77.

Reay, D. (2001) Finding or losing yourself?: Working-class relationships to education, *Journal of Educational Policy,* 16(4): 333–46.

Reay, D., Davies, J., David, M. and Ball, S. J. (2001) Choices of degree or degrees of choice? Class, race and the higher education process, *Sociology,* 35(4): 855–70.

Richter, R. (1997) The transition from secondary to higher education in Germany, *Quality in Higher Education,* 3(2): 143–53.

Ricoeur, P. (1981) *Hermeneutics and the Human Sciences.* Cambridge: Cambridge University Press.

Robertson, D. (2002) *Intermediate-level Qualifications in Higher Education: An International Assessment.* www.hefce.ac.uk/Pubs/RDreports/Downloads/report12.htm (accessed on 20 July 2003).

Rogers, C. (2002) Developing a positive approach to failure, in M. Peelo and T. Wareham (eds) *Failing Students in Higher Education,* pp. 113–23. Buckingham: Society for Research in Higher Education and Open University Press.

Rosenberg, M. and McCullough, B. C. (1981) Mattering: Inferred significance and mental health among adolescents, in R. Simmons (ed.) *Research in Community and Mental Health,* Vol. 2. Greenwich, CT: JAI Press.

Rotter, J. B. (1966) Generalized expectancies for internal versus external control of reinforcement, *Psychological Monographs 80.*

Ruppert, S. (1994) *Charting Higher Education Accountability: A Sourcebook on State-level Performance Indicators.* Denver, CO: Education Commission of the States.

Rushforth, J. (2003) Letter, *The Times Higher Education Supplement,* No. 1576, 14 February.

Salovey, P. and Mayer, J. D. (1990) Emotional intelligence, *Imagination, Cognition, and Personality,* 9: 185–211.

Sandler, M. (2000) Career decision-making self-efficacy, perceived stress, and an integrated model of student persistence: a structural model of student persistence, *Research in Higher Education,* 41(5): 537–80.

Sanford, N. (1966) *Self and Society.* New York: Atherton.

Schedvin, M. B. (1985) 'Why we discontinued': An exploration of voluntary discontinuation of studies among first year students at a college of health sciences, *Higher Education Research and Development,* 4(2): 159–73.

Schlossberg, N. K., Lynch, A. Q. and Chickering, A. W. (1989) *Improving Higher Education Environments for Adults: Responsive Programs and Services from Entry to Departure.* San Francisco: Jossey-Bass.

Schuller, T. (2000) Thinking about Social Capital. Paper presented at the Festival of Lifelong Learning Conference, University of East London, London, England, 26 July.

Schuller, T., Raffe, D., Morgan-Klein, B. and Clark, I. (1999) *Part-time Higher Education: Policy, Practice and Experience*. London: Jessica Kingsley.

Schutte, N. S. and Malouff, J. M. (2002) Incorporating emotional skills content in a college transition course enhances student retention, *Journal of the First-Year Experience*, 14(1): 7–21.

Scott, P. (1995) *The Meanings of Mass Higher Education*. Buckingham: The Society for Research into Higher Education & Open University Press.

Seligman, M. (1998) *Learned Optimism*. New York: Pocket Books.

Seymour, E. and Hewitt, N. M. (1997) *Talking about Leaving: Why Undergraduates Leave the Sciences*. Oxford: Westview Press.

Sharma, R. and Burgess, Z. (1994) Student discontinuation at a technological higher education institution, *Journal of Tertiary Education Administration*, 16(2): 225–38.

Spady, W. G. (1970) Dropouts from higher education: An interdisciplinary review and synthesis, *Interchange*, 1(1): 64–85.

Stage, F. and Anaya, G. (1996) A transformational view of college student research, in F. Stage, G. Anaya, J. Bean, D. Hossler and G. Kuh (eds) *College Students: The Evolving Nature of Research*. Boston: Pearson Custom Publishing.

Sternberg, R. J. (1997) *Successful Intelligence: How Practical and Creative Intelligence Determine Success in Life*. New York: Plume.

Sternberg, R. J. and Grigorenko, E. L. (2000) Practical intelligence and its development, in R. Bar-On and J. D. A. Parker (eds) *The Handbook of Emotional Intelligence: Theory, Development, Assessment, and Application at Home, School, and in the Workplace*, pp. 215–43. San Francisco, CA: Jossey-Bass.

Strauss, A. and Corbin, J. (1998) *Basics of Qualitative Research*, 2nd edn. California: Sage.

Thomas, L. (2002) Student retention in higher education: The role of institutional habitus, *Journal of Education Policy*, 17(4): 423–42.

Thomas, L., Woodrow, M. and Yorke, M. (2001) Access and retention, in Action on Access (2003) *Student Success in Higher Education*, pp. 35–72. Bradford: University of Bradford.

Thomas, S. L. (2000) Ties that bind: A social network approach to understanding student integration and persistence, *Journal of Higher Education*, 71(5): 591–615.

Tierney, W. G. (1992) An anthropological analysis of student participation in college, *Journal of Higher Education*, 63(6): 603–18.

Tierney, W. G. (2000) Power, identity and the dilemma of college early departure, in J. M. Braxton (ed.) *Reworking the Student Departure Puzzle*, pp. 213–34. Nashville TN: Vanderbilt University Press.

Tinto, V. (1975) Dropout from higher education; a theoretical synthesis of recent research, *Review of Educational Research*, 45(1): 89–125.

Tinto, V. (1982) Limits of theory and practice in student attrition, *Journal of Higher Education*, 53(6): 687–700.

Tinto, V. (1986) Theories of student departure revisited, in J. Smart (ed.) *Higher Education: A Handbook of Theory and Research*, Vol. 2, pp. 359–84. New York: Agathon.

Tinto, V. (1987) *Leaving College: Rethinking the Causes and Cures of Student Attrition*, 1st edn. Chicago: University of Chicago Press.

Tinto, V. (1993) *Leaving College: Rethinking the Causes and Cures of Student Attrition*, 2nd edn. Chicago: University of Chicago Press.

Tinto, V. (1997) Classroom as Communities: Exploring the Educational Character of Student Persistence, *Journal of Higher Education*, 68(6): 599–623.

Tinto, V. (2000) Linking learning and leaving, in J. M. Braxton (ed.) *Reworking the Departure Puzzle*, pp. 81–94. Nashville TN: Vanderbilt University Press.

University of Sydney (2000) *Performance-based Funding of Teaching.* www.itl.usyd.edu.au/itl/TandL/images/brochure.pdf, accessed on 19 July.

University of Sydney (2003) *Striving for Quality: Learning, Teaching & Scholarship [Draft response].* www.backingaustraliasfuture.gov.au/submissions/issues_sub/pdf/i65.pdf (accessed on 18 July).

UUK (2002a) *Social Class and Participation: Good Practice in Widening Access to Higher Education.* London: Universities UK.

UUK (2002b) *Student services: effective approaches to retaining students in higher education.* London: Universities UK.

van Gennep, A. (1908) *The Rites of Passage*, English translation edn. London: Routledge and Kegan Paul.

Wallace, W. (1971) *The Logic of Science in Sociology.* Chicago: Aldine-Atherton.

Watson, D. and Bowden, R. (1999) Why did they do it?: The Conservatives and mass higher education, 1979–97, *Journal of Educational Policy*, 14(3): 243–56.

Whitman, N. A., Spendlove, D. C. and Clark, C. H. (1984) *Student Stress: Effects and Solutions.* Washington, DC: Association for the Study of Higher Education.

Wolf, A. (2002) *Does Education Matter?: Myths about Education and Economic Growth.* London: Penguin.

Woodward, W. (2001) *Stunning U-turn on Student Grants.* www.politics.guardian.co.uk/labour2001/story/0,1414,562945,00.html (accessed on 26 May 2003).

Yorke, M. (1996) *Indicators of Programme Quality.* London: Higher Education Quality Council.

Yorke, M. (1997) A good league table guide?, *Quality Assurance in Education*, 5(2): 61–72.

Yorke, M. (1998a) Performance indicators relating to student development: can they be trusted?, *Quality in Higher Education*, 4(1): 45–61.

Yorke, M. (1998b) *The Times* 'league table' of universities, 1997: a statistical appraisal, *Quality Assurance in Education*, 6(1): 58–60.

Yorke, M. (1999a) *Getting it Right First Time.* Cheltenham: Universities and Colleges Admission Service.

Yorke, M. (1999b) *Leaving Early: Undergraduate Non-completion in Higher Education.* London: Taylor & Francis.

Yorke, M. (2000) Benchmarking the student experience, in N. Jackson and H. Lund (eds) *Benchmarking for Higher Education*, pp. 67–84. Buckingham: SRHE and Open University Press.

Yorke, M. (2001) Formative Assessment and its Relevance to Retention, *Higher Education Research and Development*, 20(2): 115–26.

Yorke, M. (2002) Academic Failure: a Retrospective View from Non-completing Students, in M. Peelo and T. Wareham (eds) *Failing Students in Higher Education*, pp. 29–44. Buckingham: The Society for Research in Higher Education and Open University Press.

Yorke, M. (2003a) Formative assessment in higher education: moves towards theory and the enhancement of pedagogic practice, *Higher Education*, 45(4): 477–501.

Yorke, M. (2003b) The Prejudicial Papers? Press Treatment of UK Higher Education Performance Indicators 1999–2001, in M. Tight (ed.) *Access and Exclusion – International Perspectives in Higher Education Research*, Vol. 2, pp. 159–84. Oxford: JAI/Elsevier Science.

Yorke, M. (2003c) *Transition into Higher Education: Some Implications for the 'Employ-ability Agenda'*. Available as *Report EMPL014*. www.ltsn.ac.uk/genericcentre/index. asp?id=18410 (accessed on 22 July 2003).

Yorke, M., Bell, R., Dove, A., Haslam, E., Hughes-Jones, H., Longden, B., O'Connell, C., Typuszak, R. and Ward, J. (1997) *Undergraduate Non-completion in Higher Education in England*, Report 97/29. Bristol: Higher Education Funding Council for England.

Yorke, M. and Knight, P. (2004) Self-theories: some implications for teaching and learning in higher education, *Studies in Higher Education*, 29 (forthcoming).

Yorke, M. and Thomas, L. (2003) Improving the retention of students from lower socio-economic groups, *Journal of Higher Education Policy and Management*, 25(1): 63–74.

Endnotes

[1] These are highly vocational programmes of two years full-time study or its equivalent.

[2] Borland (2001–2002) acknowledges that different constituencies have different interests, as regards information concerning retention. However, his 'four paradigms' are easily reducible to two, relating on one hand to the development of students and, on the other, to institutional economics.

[3] The term 'stopping out' was introduced in the US as a label for temporary withdrawal, and is equivalent to the terms 'suspension' or 'intercalation' of studies in the UK. 'Stopping out' is more likely to occur where students suffer economic stress and/or have responsibilities in respect of others.

[4] The 'Student Progress Unit' (see, for example, Dobson et al. 1996 and Chapter 3, p. 53)

[5] Dweck (1999) would perhaps construe these self-reflections in terms of orientations towards learning or performance: we deal further with this issue in Chapter 6.

[6] Though there are often instruments that measure them in the abstract.

[7] Readers wishing to pursue this aspect of student success may find the following to be of interest: materials on the Learning and Teaching Support Network's website (*www.ltsn.ac.uk/ESECT*), and Knight and Yorke (2003, 2004).

[8] They do not have to pass the year-end assessments, since if funding were dependent on passing there would be pressure on academic standards.

[9] *http://nces.ed.gov.*

[10] This implies that the earlier estimate by Yorke et al. (1997) was low. This apparent underestimate may reflect the fact that the HESA data of that time were more unreliable than supposed: the data for the years covered by Yorke and colleagues' study derived from a data-collection system that had yet to be fully 'bedded in'.

[11] There is a similar concern in New Zealand to engage the Maori population more extensively in higher education (Ministry of Education 2002: 29–35).

[12] A speech by the then Secretary of State for Education was particularly influential (Baker 1989).

[13] The Scottish and Welsh approaches are conveniently summarized in House of Commons (2002: paras 39–45).

[14] Bourdieu (1973) would interpret this in terms of the acquisition of cultural capital.

[15] See *www.higheredinfo.org* (accessed on 20 July 2003).

[16] See the website of the National Center for Higher Education Management Systems [NCHEMS] at *www.nchems.org*.

[17] Tennessee was a pioneer in this respect, commencing its approach in 1979 (see Banta 1988). For a more recent review of performance-based funding, see Ewell (1999).

[18] Source: Department of Education (2002a).

[19] That is, school pupils entering with scores analogous to the A Level points score used in England, Wales and Northern Ireland.

[20] Another 'uneasy triangle' links research, teaching and public service.

[21] Parliament uses the Select Committee structure to call the executive to account for policy. Each State Office has its own Select Committee comprising backbenchers who have the authority to call ministers, civil servants and other expert witnesses before them to answer questions on matters related to policy.

[22] Most of this expansion took place in the polytechnics and colleges rather than in the then universities (Scott 1995).

[23] Kenneth Baker's speech at Lancaster University is widely claimed to have been a driver for the expansion in the early 1990s (Baker 1989). For a further discussion, see Watson and Bowden (1999).

[24] House of Commons (2001c: viii).

[25] Students who lived away from home – typical in UK higher education – attracted a greater amount of state support than did their home-based peers.

[26] Later these were taken over by the Quality Assurance Agency for Higher Education (QAA).

[27] See House of Commons (2001c: 62, para. 195).

[28] The projected impact of the options on high and low income families was summarized in NCIHE (1997: para. 20.57).

[29] These data (which are derived from statistics on the DfES website) refer to A-Level results in 2001, at the level of the local education authority. They are reported more fully in Yorke (2003c).

[30] Parts of the south-west, particularly Cornwall, also suffer from economic stress.

[31] HEFCE was probably alluding to this study in a memorandum to the Select Committee (see House of Commons 2001b: 87, para. 10). In a few schools, pupils from independent schools did outperform their state-educated counterparts.

[32] See House of Commons (2001c: xvi, para. 39ff).

[33] The 'postcode premium' is acknowledged as an imprecise instrument, and the Education and Skills Select Committee recommended that a more refined methodology be developed.

[34] Additional resources might be acquired from sources other than the public purse, but acquiring these is likely to be harder for those institutions that are particularly successful in widening access, since they tend not to have the attracting power of the elite institutions.

[35] And as the Education and Skills Select Committee appreciates (House of Commons 2003: para. 136).

[36] A speech delivered at London Guildhall University (Morris 2001).

[37] There is a 60–40 split between the two groups in contemporary Great Britain (House of Commons 2001c: 19), showing a shift towards non-manual occupations since HEFCE published its first set of performance indicators.

[38] In an early study Johnes used as an index whether the student had completed their programme at the end of the sixth year after enrolment, but this makes no

allowance for the variation in the nominal course duration. In contrast, Astin et al. (1996) took nine years as a 'cut-off' criterion, and Gaither et al. (1994) suggested the criterion of half as long again as the nominal course duration.

[39] See NAB Good Management Practice Group (1987).

[40] A distinction that was not entirely logical, since universities also were in receipt of substantial public funding.

[41] See Cave et al. (1997: 124ff) and Yorke (1998a).

[42] Data on research performance are also included, but are not considered here.

[43] The data for completion are *estimates* based on previous performance, and not absolute values.

[44] Johnes and Taylor (1990) had found that institutional characteristics could account for variation in the performance of the then university sector in the UK.

[45] The 2002 publication includes a location-adjusted benchmark.

[46] These statistics do not include adjustments related to the particular characteristics of individual institutions. An analysis on a UK-wide basis would produce a very similar pattern of statistics. The focus is on England because the research reported in this chapter relates to English higher education.

[47] Socio-economic groups IIIm, IV and V can be loosely interpreted as 'working class'.

[48] 'Mature' entrants to full-time programmes are those who enter at age 21 or above.

[49] See Knight and Yorke (2003) for data that suggest this.

[50] These institutions have not been included in Table 5.2 on the grounds of their atypicality.

[51] This is a crude form of standardization which lacks the methodological robustness of a z-score.

[52] The CEQ has a number of technical weaknesses: see Yorke (1996: 196–201).

[53] This section is based on Yorke (2003b).

[54] See, on the debt issue, Callender and Kemp (2000) and UUK (2002a). Callender (2003) also deals with potential higher education students' attitudes to debt.

[55] 'Sandwich' programmes – elsewhere termed 'co-operative education programmes' – incorporate a period of placement in an employment-relevant environment. The norm in the UK is for this to be a year in length.

[56] See Yorke (2000) for some practical examples of benchmarking as applied to the student experience.

[57] No doubt for both altruistic and self-interested reasons.

[58] The use of the word 'in' rather than 'by' is deliberate, since it allows for the possibility that the behaviour of a student's peers may influence the choice between persistence and departure.

[59] An illustration of cultural capital was provided by 'Seven-up', a television programme transmitted in the UK in the late 1960s. This programme was based on interviews with children from a broad social background about a variety of issues. One group interview with four bright 7-year-olds, sitting on a couch in their London public school, was particularly vivid. Each was able to discuss not only plans for the immediate future, but also long-term plans for university. Their planning was detailed even down to the name of the Oxbridge college and the subject they would read. They were sophisticated and knowledgeable at age 7. On being re-interviewed some 21 years later their original perceptions of the future turned out to be as they had predicted.

[60] The model (Bean and Eaton 2000: 57) appears to suggest that these changes are positive, but this is not necessarily the case.

[61] Gloria and Robinson Kurpius (2001) note the significance of self-beliefs along with social support and 'comfort' for the persistence of American Indian under-graduates.

[62] To be fair, there are hints to be found scattered throughout Tinto (1993: Chapter 5).

[63] Pintrich (2000) subdivides performance goals into 'approach' and 'avoidance' varieties. 'Approach' performance goals relate to a person's striving to excel (and can be effective in producing results), whereas the 'avoidance' variety relates to a person not wishing to be seen to perform badly (and is generally not conducive to learning).

[64] Cabrera et al. (1992: 144), commenting on Tinto's earlier writings (Tinto 1975, 1982, 1986) and allied research, note that the importance of external factors in shaping students' perceptions, commitments and preferences is overlooked. They point out that external factors are 'particularly relevant from policy as well as institutional perspectives, given the different social and institutional programs aimed at stimulating enrolment and preventing attrition by addressing variables other than institutional ones (that is, ability to pay, parental support)'.

[65] However, some variables may be quite highly correlated, in which case the problem of (multi-)collinearity can render analyses problematic. For a discussion of this issue, see Pedhazur (1997: 294ff).

[66] As also do Metzner and Bean (1987) with their 29 per cent of the variance explained. Cabrera et al. (1992) obtained slightly higher proportions of the variance in persistence explained by two causal models they were investigating, 38 and 44 per cent.

[67] Further examples can be found in Harvey et al. (1961) and Bakan (1967).

[68] The delineation of factors that influence academic integration, however, is unwarranted despite the central role academic integration plays in Tinto's Inter-actionalist Theory. Because fewer than two-thirds of empirical tests find that academic integration wields a positive influence on subsequent commitment to the goal of graduation from college (Braxton et al. 1997), on subsequent commitment to the institution (Braxton and Lien 2000), and on student departure (Braxton and Lien 2000), we assert that academic integration plays an inconsistent role in the student departure process (Braxton et al. 1997; Braxton and Lien 2000).

[69] This is not to assert that qualitative studies are 'better' than quantitative studies. They address the issues in different ways, and can be seen as complementary. A methodological difficulty, though, is that relatively rarely are substantial quantitative studies augmented by qualitative detail, meaning that evidence has to be compiled from different studies undertaken in different circumstances.

[70] Sandwich programmes incorporate periods of work placement, typically of a year's duration. In the US and Ireland, the term 'co-operative education' is used for such programmes.

[71] Some of this was acknowledged in Yorke (1999b).

[72] This work was undertaken by a team from the north-west of England and a substantial part of it was published as Yorke et al. (1997).

[73] However, some quantitative longitudinal studies, such as those by Cabrera et al. (1992) and Braxton et al. (1995), appear in the US literature on retention.

[74] Six institutions were involved in this survey: two 'old' universities; two 'new' universities; and two colleges of higher education.

[75] Apparently, students from arid countries can be surprised by the climate of the UK when they arrive.

[76] See, for example, McGuire (1995); Morrison et al. (1995); Yorke (1997, 1998a); Bowden (2000).

[77] These are available on the QAA website (*www.qaa.ac.uk*) and in hard copy.

[78] These surveys attracted 4028 and 2609 responses, respectively.

[79] See Yorke (1999b: 131–2).

[80] The analysis on which this is based can be found in Yorke (2002).

[81] The fee contribution was means-tested, so that students from the poorest backgrounds paid nothing.

[82] See Callender and Kemp (2000) in respect of the UK, and McInnis et al. (2000) in respect of Australia.

[83] The reliability of these data is problematic since accuracy in reporting is difficult to achieve, especially when reliance is placed on retrospection. That many students work a considerable number of hours in part-time employment is not a matter for dispute.

[84] It is impossible to determine whether this is a methodological artefact, resulting from differences between the employed and non-employed respondents. Barke et al. (2000: 48) discuss briefly differences between subject areas, but are hampered in their analysis by small numbers once their sample is disaggregated. There are, however, hints that the difference might be associated with timetabled hours: subject areas where these are typically higher may experience student absence from time-tabled sessions, and in the arts, humanities and social sciences there may be greater scope for students to keep up by reading relevant materials. The difference in mean mark between employed students and those not in part-time employment ranged between +0.6 and −1.6 percentage points for years 1, 3 and 4.

[85] The new universities in the UK have a long-established tradition of part-time higher education.

[86] See *www.hesa.co.uk/holisdocs/pubinfo/student/subject0102.htm* (accessed 21 July 2003).

[87] The study of part-time higher education in Scotland by Schuller et al. (1999) provides useful insights into the experience of students, but does not deal with the issue of completion.

[88] The focus is on England because the research reported in this chapter relates to English higher education.

[89] The discrepancy from the benchmark figure is only flagged in the HEFCE tables when the performance figure is at least three standard deviations and also at least three percentage points from the benchmark. Smaller differences are considered not to be sufficient to merit flagging.

[90] At that time other demographic indicators that might have a bearing on insti-tutional performance, such as student ethnicity and the geographical location of the institution, were not included in the published tables.

[91] This account is based upon Yorke and Thomas (2003).

[92] The policy concern has really been related to the over-representation of pupils from the fee-paying schools in the UK in what have been termed the 'top uni-versities'. The citing of the percentage from state schools is a coded way of referring to what is believed to be a selection bias in the higher education system.

[93] Maggie Woodrow and Liz Thomas, joined by Mantz Yorke. Sadly, Maggie Woodrow died during the course of the project.

[94] The vignettes can be found in Thomas et al. (2001).

[95] Callender and Kemp (2000) found that religious considerations might preclude some students from taking up loans, which offers a challenge to policies promoting equality of opportunity.

[96] See Newby's comment to this effect in House of Commons (2001c: 62, para. 198). McInnis (2001) makes a similar point in relation to the Australian context.

[97] Pascarella and Terenzini (1991) noted the benefit to US students from on-campus, compared with off-campus, employment.

[98] This account draws upon work conducted by Layer et al. (2002).

[99] 'Trading up' the reputational range by students is not unknown, and is a problem for some institutions.

[100] It is the norm for the first year of full-time study in England, Wales and Northern Ireland to be treated as a qualifying year for the honours-level programme. In effect, a student merely has to pass the first year assessments to qualify, since the gradings for the first year do not carry forward.

[101] The possibility of a less noble influence cannot be discounted. Early failure can be sufficiently discouraging to students that they leave, with adverse consequences for institutional performance statistics relating to retention.

[102] We contrast our approach to making suggestions (based on theory and empirical findings) with that of Moxley et al. (2001) who surprisingly make no overt appeal to the literature.

[103] Berger (2001–2002); Braxton and McClendon (2001–2002); Bean and Eaton (2000); Kuh (2001–2002); Nora (2001–2002).

[104] *www.ucas.ac.uk.*

[105] Though note that students may select an institution into which they will feel personally comfortable, consistently with Bourdieu's theorizing on social structure. Examples can be found in Reay et al. (2001) and Read et al. (2003).

[106] The Department for Education and Skills envisages that the further expansion in England will be based on Foundation Degrees (DfES 2003a), but their take-up will depend on a number of factors including perceived value, employer valuation, and cost. These programmes are intended to mitigate the interim qualification gap, corresponding broadly to the Associate Degree in the US and to a variety of diploma-level qualifications in Europe. Robertson (2002) provides an overview of international practice as regards intermediate qualifications.

[107] See also Example 7 in NAO (2002a: 29).

[108] This is a familiar practice in the US, and some institutions in the UK have adopted it. However, in Germany the expectation is that students are mature enough to act as independent agents (Richter 1997).

[109] However, the possibility of a 'Hawthorne effect' cannot be discounted.

[110] A fuller treatment of formative assessment is given in Knight and Yorke (2003: Chapters 3 and 9).

[111] Pre-entry workshops will probably fail to cater for students who enter an institution at the last minute.

[112] Clearing is a system operated by the Universities and Colleges Admission Service to enable students who failed to secure a place in higher education following the publication of the Advanced Level examination in mid-August to be considered by those institutions with places unfilled. As noted in the text the period between publication of examination results and the start of the academic year is less than four weeks (shorter in some cases) which puts considerable pressure on the student and institution to complete all the necessary pre-entry administration.

[113] In the early stages of science-based programmes, greater weight might be given to the student's demonstration that they 'know the basics'.

[114] Save by the student filing for bankruptcy – but this has serious consequences for future financial activity, such as gaining credit, or taking out a mortgage.

[115] 'Above average teaching is a non-negotiable criterion for success' (University of Sydney 2003: 2).

[116] Predictable retention also helps institutions to manage their finances.

Author Index

Subject index

RESEARCHING HIGHER EDUCATION
ISSUES AND APPROACHES

Malcolm Tight

This book couples an authoritative overview of the principal current areas of research into higher education with a guide to the core methods used for researching higher education. It offers both a configuration of research on higher education, as seen through the lens of methodology, and suggestions for further research.

Contents

Case studies and tables are separately listed after the main contents pages – Part I: Recently Published Research on Higher Education – Introduction – Journals – Books – Part II: Issues and Approaches in Researching Higher Education – Researching Teaching and Learning – Researching Course Design – Researching the Student Experience – Researching Quality – Researching System Policy – Researching Institutional Management – Researching Academic Work – Researching Knowledge – Part III: The Process of Researching Higher Education – Method and Methodology in Researching Higher Education – Researching Higher Education at Different Levels – The Process of Researching – References

417pp   0 335 21117 8 (Paperback)   0 335 21118 6 (Hardback)

HIGHER EDUCATION AND THE LIFECOURSE

Maria Slowey and David Watson (Eds.)

As we enter the twenty-first century it is increasingly clear to professionals at all levels of formal and informal education that we need to refresh the concept of lifelong learning. Most importantly, the concept needs to be expanded so that it is lifelong and lifewide, concerned not just with serial requirements of those already engaged, but also with the creation of opportunities for those who have not found the existing structures and processes accessible or useful.

The volume is structured around resulting arguments about policy and practice in three parts. The first focuses on the lifelong dimension, addressing in particular the changing nature of the student population. The second investigates the lifewide connections between higher education and other areas of social and economic life. The final section draws together a structural analysis, as well as research on changing needs of learners, to set out some key implications for higher education.

Contents

417pp   0 335 21377 4 (Paperback)   0 335 21378 2 (Hardback)

ASSESSMENT, LEARNING AND EMPLOYABILITY

Peter Knight and Mantz Yorke

"Knight and Yorke argue that our assessment practices are often not able to meet students' governments' and employers' expectations. We need to reconsider how higher education can judge and describe students' achievements. This is 'a thinking person's guide to assessment' which makes a compelling case that the challenges facing higher education demand radical changes in assessment thinking, and not mere tinkering with methods."

Peggi Maki, American Association for Higher Education

What is assessed gets attention: what is not assessed does not. When Higher education is expected to promote complex achievements in subject disciplines and in terms of 'employability', problems arise: how are such achievements to be assessed?

In the first part, it is argued that existing grading practices cannot cope with the expectations laid upon them, while the potential of formative assessment for the support of learning is not fully realised. The authors argue that improving the effectiveness of assessment depends on a well-grounded appreciation of what assessment is, and what may and may not be expected of it.

The second part is about summative judgements for high-stakes purposes. Using established measurement theory, a view is developed of the conditions under which affordable, useful, valid and reliable summative judgements can be made. One conclusion is that many complex achievements resist high-stakes assessment, which directs attention to low-stakes, essentially formative, alternatives. Assessment for learning and employability demands more than module-level changes to assessment methods.

The text concludes with a discussion of how institutions can respond in policy terms to the challenges that have been posed.

Assessment, Learning and Employability has wide and practical relevance – to teachers, module and programme leaders, higher education managers and quality enhancement specialists.

Contents: *Preface – Higher education and employability – Summative assessment in disarray – Formative assessment: unrealized potential – Key themes in thinking about assessment – Diversifying assessment methods – Assessing for employability – Authenticity in assessment – Optimizing the reliability of assessment – Making better use of formative assessment – Progression – Claims making – Assessment systems in academic departments – Developing the institutional assessment system – Conclusions.*

c.224pp   0 335 21228 X (Paperback)   0 335 21229 8 (Hardback)